"My beloved is white and ruddy, the chiefest among ten thousand. His head is as the most fine gold, his locks are bushy, and black as a raven. His eyes are as the eyes of doves by the rivers of waters, washed with milk, and fitly set. His cheeks are as a bed of spices, as sweet flowers: his lips like lilies, dropping sweet smelling myrrh. His hands are as gold rings set with the beryl: his belly is as bright ivory overlaid with sapphires. His legs are as pillars of marble, set upon sockets of fine gold: his countenance is as Lebanon, excellent as the cedars. His mouth is most sweet: yea, he is Muhammad."

To he without whom there would be no established sky, nor an outstretched Earth, nor an illuminated Moon, nor a glowing Sun, nor a rotating cosmos, nor a flowing sea, nor a sailing ship.

Table of Contents

Preface

✳✳✳

This life is a journey. Our ship leaves the shore in calm waters, but as we sail further into the ocean, we experience storms, darkness, and starvation on the ship. But if we are creative, strong, and patient, we can make our way through the collapsing waves, and back again onto the shore. We begin this life as naïve, innocent children. Then, we grow into maturity, and experience hardship and confusion. This causes us to seek an understanding of our world and ourselves. We continue that development until we return to peace.

This is a particularly tough time for the Muslim world, which has been submerged into all forms of crisis. But our tradition is a lifeboat, and it is a source of stability amidst many extremes. I've come to appreciate the beauty of tradition over the utility of modernity, the Ark over the Titanic – but I also believe that beauty and utility can be reconciled and were never meant to be mutually exclusive. Order is ultimately both. Ethics is but a branch of aesthetics, and justice is putting everything in its rightful place.

My name is Bilal, and I am not a scholar or shaykh. I am just your brother. I am a teacher, translator, researcher, writer and poet. I have devoted much of my life to the study of religion. What I've always liked about Islam is that it is a sophisticated, full-circle, holistic, and comprehensive worldview and way of life. It never leaves one without guidance, on nearly every aspect of one's life, from the mundane to the sacred. How to make the best out of life and society is all delineated in a relatively clear and consistent way.

Some may find that constricting, but order is the highest function of human life, in that our minds incline towards order (categorization, systematization, theorization, discipline, cleanliness, organization, language, and logic). These are some of man's highest expressions, and we feel dissatisfied with confusion, disorganization, and laziness. Ethics is but a branch of aesthetics, and in order and symmetry we find beauty and peace. Despite its vast complexity, Islam appealed to every part of the world, and was practiced closely and consistently for many centuries, which suggests that the regimen it brings is constructed to fit human nature and human convention. It is a robust tradition in a world that is constantly changing to the whims of the masses and the market.

The Quran inspired a cultural, philosophical, scientific, and legal revolution. *Jahl* and Jāhilīyya is the lowest state that a human being and a society can be in. I've never encountered a tradition or worldview that despises ignorance as much as Islam does. It never left me without answers, and the higher I wanted to go, the more this tradition would overwhelm me with detail and meaning.

The struggle of all people today is a spiritual struggle. Many of us achieved material success, travelled the world, and sought life's pleasures. Human ingenuity has brought extraordinary technology to our fingertips. But despite this, we struggle with high rates of depression, anxiety, trauma, addiction, and suicide. Something about the modern world is crushing our spirits, causing us to seek consumer anesthetics. Reflecting on these concerns is what led me to writing this book as a reminder to myself, my loved ones, and anyone else that may benefit.

The title, "All the Perfumes of Arabia", comes from Shakespeare's *Macbeth*. Lady Macbeth says that "all the perfumes of Arabia" would not cover up the stench of her bloody crime. Indeed, Arabia was well-known for trading precious scents used for both medicinal and practical purposes. The Prophet Muḥammad ﷺ in particular loved fragrances.

Aromatherapy is the use of fragrant essential oils for therapeutic purposes. Scents are known to uplift moods are remove stress. The Prophet ﷺ would anoint his head, beard, and face with essential oils, and he was known for his musky aroma. He would breathe in these scents as he would apply them. Hence, this book uses twelve popular scents and connects their symbolism to various self-help themes. My hope is that this unique approach inspires the reader to look at his or her problems in a different light.

May Allah aid us in healing ourselves and others.

حسبي الله ونعم الوكيل

Allah is sufficient for me, for He is the best trustee.

Chapter 1

Amber: Extolling the Excellence of Allah

***

Praise be to Allah, the One who is sought when all hope is lost. Praise be to Allah, who is manifest, but not to sight. He is remote, but not in distance. He is near, but not in reach. Time cannot contain Him, space cannot encompass Him, descriptions cannot restrict Him, and writings cannot comprehend Him. He is the Unique, the Besought of All: He does not beget, and He was not begotten. He has no partners: all things are unlike Him and He is unlike all things. Imagination falls short of reaching Him. He is the Originator of all that exists, and His creation is wholly contingent upon Him. Allah is One, but not in enumeration. He is the Creator, but not through labour. He is the First who is beyond beginnings, the Last who is beyond endings, and the everlasting who is beyond the likeness of all created things.

Allah's mercy prevails over His wrath (إِنَّ رَحْمَتِي غَلَبَتْ غَضَبِي). Allah's foremost names are the Absolutely Merciful, the Especially Merciful (الرحمن الرحيم). The word *rahm* means womb, as Allah is our Sustainer and Nurturer (رب). His mercy embraces all things (7:156), while His punishment does not. The Messenger of Allah ﷺ was sent as the Mercy to the Worlds (رحمة للعالمين). Despite the debauchery of his people, who were at the edge of destruction (3:103), he did not give up on them.

Nobody gives like Allah! The most hateful sound to God is the braying of an ass (31:19). We bray and complain over small things, when we have been given a chance to see the majesty of this world with our eyes. We have been given a chance to hear the unique sound of every creature with our ears. We have been given a chance to express our complex thoughts and feelings. The universe and its knowledge are inexhaustible, so keep discovering His signs and know that He is the Creator and Sustainer of all things.

God never "blocks" you – you can always find Him. He accepts every "follow" request, even if you "unfollowed"

Him before. Despite having billions of likes, you can speak directly to Him and He will listen to you. He has no pictures, but He is the most beautiful. Don't treat God the way you would treat a winter coat. You put on a coat when it is cold, and then you forget about it when the season has changed. God is not just there when you need Him, He is there when you are compromising Him and forgetting Him.

The word *dīn* (دين) is often translated as "religion", or "way of life". The word is closely related to the word *dayn* (دَين) which means debt, liability, and obligation; and the word *dān* (دان): to be subject to someone.

This helps us understand the verse in Surat al-Fātiha, where God is described as Master of the Day of Requital (literally, the day of *dīn*). The Day of Judgment is the day where we must pay back all our dues. We are indebted to Allah, the one who gave us life, sustenance and guidance. We were given the opportunity to know Him and His marvels without even asking for it. So, Islam (submission to Allah) is the due that is paid in gratitude.

Tawḥīd is often translated as "monotheism", but it is actually a verbal noun that roughly translates to "the making of one". It is the process by which one expunges his self of the many gods that he worships: man-made deities, appetites, tyrannical hierarchies, and the ego. The process is continual, and it culminates with our last breath.

Shirk is often translated as "polytheism", but in reality, few people believe in multiple, distinct, co-eternal gods. Even the Arabs of Jāhilīyya recognized Allah as the creator of the heavens and the Earth (31:25). The *ilāh* in Arabic is that which is obeyed (*ma'lūh*). *Shirk* in its truest sense is obeying anything at the expense of the obedience to God. One may obey their appetites, their desires, their ruler, their boss, their parents, their tribe, their culture, or even their religious leader in opposition to God. The object of Islam is to give Allah a monopoly on authority, and to submit fully to Him. As soon as we associate partners with Him, then we miss the most fundamental truth of our existence, and we create disorder and chaos in ourselves and around us.

All sins are rooted in some form of *shirk*. When Iblīs refused to bow to Adam, his envy was rooted in a sense of entitlement. Even though he was worshiping Allah for thousands of years, he was worshiping Allah for his own sake – to be God's beloved chosen one. Iblīs not only disobeyed Allah but disagreed with His choice and debated Him. Iblīs therefore preferred himself over God, out of arrogance, and this is a form of *shirk*.

Iblīs let his religiosity make him feel that he had a right over God. His dedication made him feel entitled to a position that was not made for him. His worship was egocentric, and he was overcome with jealousy when he was not validated. How many of us are guilty of worshiping the way Iblīs worshiped? Woe to those who gain an iota of gnosis yet feel that they are better than their brothers and sisters in faith. Until we realize that we are poor slaves, who know only as much Allah allows, and who worship only as much as Allah provides His support, we will be subject to fall all the way down as Iblīs fell.

11

In 9:31 in the Quran, the people were described as taking their rabbis and priests as lords besides Allah. This was not because they bowed down to their rabbis. This was because, according to the exegeses, the people obeyed their rabbis at the expense of obeying God and His Messenger. A role model and guide will either lead to you Allah or Satan; and following Satan is *shirk*, even if it is done by a technical "monotheist". Hence, *tawhīd* is not just belief in God's Oneness, which even a Deist accepts, but it is recognizing God's authority, aligning with Him, and preferring His will over all other things.

The prevalent problem today in the modern secular world is not blind obedience to priests and rabbis. The main problem now is the heedless obedience to one's own whims – a radical version of individual agency and personal freedom that allows a person to avoid responsibilities, lack a substantive moral compass, and lack an objective truth claim. This is why we see such fluidity in moral views over very short periods of time. The lines of what is right and wrong, appropriate and inappropriate keep shifting in accordance to what the state, the market, and the whims of the people desire. We all really need to renew our *shahada* and actualize it. Praise be to Him who forgives the minor forms of *shirk* when we return to Him in repentance.

"Islam" in Arabic is the peace that comes as a result of submission. It is the admission of our dependency on and our dues to the One God. It is the acknowledgement of Him and His attributes. But we don't just stay at Islam, we grow into *Imān*. *Imān*, which is often translated as "faith", is a verbal noun closely related to the word for "safety" (*amān* أمان). It is also related to the word "entrust" (*emmin* أمّن). The faithful is called a *mu'min* because he entrusts himself to Allah, so Allah gives him safety in the Hereafter.

After that trust develops, the believer enters *Taqwā*. *Taqwā* is the feeling of wariness from danger. You watch over yourself as though you see God, because you know that He sees you. You understand the danger of temptation and sin, and so you avoid it like an engulfing fire. Then the believer enters into *Yaqīn*. *Yaqīn* is to have knowledge, gnosis, and certainty. It is to simply know the fact of your existence and to know this world and the Hereafter. It is to know God like you know your self.

Then, the believer enters *Iḥsān*. *Iḥsān* is to "make good". It is to beautify your surroundings. It is to have an aura of order and goodness, where nothing but good emanates from you. Your words and deeds are a presuppositionless reflection of the will of God.

Amber is a heavy, resinous scent. It has a warmth that permeates and pervades. Likewise, the presence of Allah is auspicious, and His praise fills the heaven and Earth.

We are wandering, on this blue marble in space, looking for perfection. We seek it in our appearance, our grades, our power, our status, our spouse, our children; but we all – sooner or later – realize that Perfection lies only in Him alone. Praise be to Allah.

Chapter 2

Musk: A Whiff of Prophetic Life

***

Picture yourself in the middle of a desert. It is rough, dry, and dusty. The Sun burns your skin, and the cloudless sky produces no shade. It is almost barren, and there is very little life. Suddenly, you find a date palm with fresh dates on it. The dates are sweet, juicy, and nourishing. You are amazed that something so delightful and so healthy could grow in such an arid place.

The Prophet Muḥammad ﷺ was born in 570 CE. Before he was born, his father had died. When he was six years of age, his mother also died. He was then taken in by his grandfather, who died two years later. Muḥammad ﷺ was then finally taken in by his uncle Abu Ṭālib. Our Messenger ﷺ was an orphan, yet he did not complain about his childhood or his omen. He made the absolute best out of his tough circumstances.

Muḥammad ﷺ belonged to the prominent family of Banu Hāshim in the city of Mecca. At the centre of Mecca was the Kāʿba, a holy cube-shaped temple dedicated to the worship of the One God, built by Abraham and Ishmael. After Abraham, 360 idols of other gods were brought into the temple, and Arabs from all over the peninsula would make pilgrimage to the Kāʿba regularly.

Muḥammad ﷺ was born in a time of Ignorance (Jāhilīyya) in Mecca. He became a merchant and was known by the title "The Truthful and the Trustworthy" (as-Sādiq al-Amīn). He resolved tribal disputes. He was well-known for his good character and his humility. When the Prophet Muḥammad ﷺ was 20, he played an instrumental role in founding the League of the Virtuous (Ḥilf al-Fuḍūl). This was a collective action committee designed to correct injustices and help powerless people. After the 4-year Fijār war, the Meccans saw firsthand that grievances can cause instability and conflict. Hence, the League would collectively intervene in conflicts to establish justice. What an example for 20-year-olds today!

His reputation attracted the attention of Khadīja, an older businesswoman and widow, who then proposed to

Muḥammad ﷺ and the two got married. Khadīja was the only woman to bear Muḥammad's children. While Khadīja was alive, Muḥammad ﷺ did not marry anyone else; and she was the most beloved of his wives. A woman knows her husband inside-out: so as soon as Muḥammad ﷺ received his first revelation, she would bear witness to his honesty and be among the first to accept his message.

Prophet Muḥammad ﷺ was a man of medium build, medium complexion, from the middle of the world, with wavy hair (neither straight nor curly), and a symmetrical body. He spoke succinctly. He was the epitome of moderation, the manifestation of the Middle Way, the head of the Middle Nation (*ummatun wasaṭ*).

It is reported that Anas, a companion of the Prophet, said, "The Messenger of Allah ﷺ had a pinkish hue. His sweat was like pearls. When he walked, he would lean forward. I have never felt brocade nor silk that was softer than his hand. I have never smelt musk nor ambergris that was sweeter than his fragrance."[1]

It is reported that Lady Fatima, the daughter of the Prophet, said, "I was looking at him, and his face was

---

كَانَ رَسُولُ اللَّهِ صلى الله عليه وسلم أَزْهَرَ اللَّوْنِ كَأَنَّ عَرَقَهُ اللُّؤْلُؤُ إِذَا ¹ مَشَى تَكَفَّأَ وَلاَ مَسِسْتُ دِيبَاجَةً وَلاَ حَرِيرَةً أَلْيَنَ مِنْ كَفِّ رَسُولِ اللَّهِ صلى الله عليه وسلم وَلاَ شَمَمْتُ مِسْكَةً وَلاَ عَنْبَرَةً أَطْيَبَ مِنْ رَائِحَةِ رَسُولِ اللَّهِ صلى الله عليه وسلم .

glittering as though it was the moon on the night of its fullness and perfection."[2]

The Messenger of Allah was a handsome man with broad shoulders, a wide chest, clear skin, a full head of hair, white teeth, curved eyebrows, and strength. Yet, Allah only complimented his character in the Quran, "Surely, you are of tremendous character." (68:4)

People worshiped idols and icons of false gods made of wood and stone. Men buried their daughters alive. Orphans and widows were abandoned. Societies were divided by tribalism and racism. Public drunkenness and nakedness were the norm. All in all, there was no sense of accountability in Arabia – there was only foolishness, humiliation, disunity, and darkness. Out of that darkness came a new light. Muḥammad ﷺ announced his prophethood at the age of 40 after experiencing supernatural encounters with the Angel Gabriel. Gabriel gradually revealed the verses of the Noble Qur'an to the Prophet over a 23-year period.

The Quran is the revelation (*tanzīl*) sent down to us by God, while the Sunna (applied praxis of the Prophet) is the elevation (*ta'wīl*) sent up from us to God. They are part of the same reality but applied in different directions. The Quran contains the principles and orders, while the Sunna contains the praxis and application.

وَصِرْتُ انظُرُ إِلَيْهِ وَإِذَا وَجْهُهُ يَتَلَالَا كَأَنَّهُ ٱلْبَدْرُ فِي لَيْلَةِ تَمَامِهِ وَكَمَالِهِ. 2

The first three revelations of Prophet Muḥammad ﷺ were "read!" (96:1), "arise to pray the night" (73:2), and "arise and warn" (74:2). This process reflects the need for Muslims to (1) devote themselves to learning, (2) practice what they have learned, and (3) call others to enjoin in established virtues and forbid evil. Likewise, the Prophet taught that there were three forms of knowledge: "Surely knowledge is three, and anything other than that is superfluous: a firm sign, a just obligation, an established Sunna."[3] The command to read corresponds to studying the signs of God (*ayāt*). The command to practice corresponds to fulfilling your ethical obligations. The command to call others corresponds to the praxis of establishing Islam in our families, institutions, and societies. Islamic practice can be summarized into this three-step process. Without one of these three tenets, the entire structure collapses.

Some amateur academics think that the Quran tells us very little about the Prophet Muḥammad ﷺ. They argue that the stories of the prophets are disparate details that were concocted and put together. But in reality, the Quran creates a dialectic that simultaneously fits all the prophets mentioned, who are all in some way analogous to the Prophet Muḥammad ﷺ and the early Muslims. Hence, early on, the idea that the Prophet was the "Speaking Quran" or "Walking Quran" was espoused. He was the fulfillment and elevation (*ta'wīl*) of the revelation.

إِنَّمَا الْعِلْمُ ثَلَاثَةٌ : آيَةٌ مُحْكَمَةٌ ، وَ فَرِيضَةٌ عَادِلَةٌ ، وَ سُنَّةٌ قَائِمَةٌ ؛ وَ مَا خَلَا «³

. « هُنَّ فَهُوَ فَضْلٌ

When we read Noah, Hūd, Ṣāliḥ, Jethro, Lot, and others in the Quran, we are to read in the subtext: Muḥammad, Muḥammad, Muḥammad ﷺ.

The Quran is unlike the Bible in that the Bible is a testament of prophecy, while the Quran is a testament of fulfillment. Muḥammad ﷺ was the foundational prophet (*nabī al-ummī*) who had all the knowledge, virtues, and authority of his predecessors. The final prophet would be the headliner, the principal act; and all the prophetic stories would parallel his own life.

Muḥammad ﷺ was ordered to warn his people that they would be judged on their faith, their deeds, and their sins. He pushed to bring social order and accountability to an ignorant, oppressive people. He was a defender of the orphans and the widows, a freer of slaves, and a friend of the poor.

Abu Dharr, an apostle of the Prophet Muḥammad ﷺ, came from a tribe that was notorious for raiding caravans. But as soon as he met this man ﷺ, he was moved to become a lover of the poor, and an honest, fearless, and empathetic man. He said, "The Messenger of Allah advised me to look to those below me and not to look to those above me. He advised me to love the poor and to love their nearness. He advised me to speak the truth, even if it is bitter. He advised me to connect with my blood-relatives, even if they turn away. He advised me not to fear the blaming of the blamer. And he advised me to increase in the saying, 'There is no power nor strength except in Allah, the High, the Great (*lā ḥawla wa lā quwwata illā billāh al-ʿalī al-ʿathīm*)', for it is from the treasures of Paradise."[4]

This is the story of so many companions – meeting the Prophet ﷺ inspired them to become dutiful and compassionate people for life. We meet few people in our lives who have such a permanent impact on who we are, yet Muḥammad's character changed the whole world.

The reformative power of our religion is something that many Muslims are forgetting. We often neglect and ostracize other Muslims for their marital status, education, poverty and past crimes or sins. One must remember that the Prophet Muḥammad ﷺ never walked away from his people, despite the debauchery that they took part in in Jāhilīyya. He never gave up on them despite the ugliness of their sins. Instead, he was a mercy to the worlds – let's try to emulate that.

In the early years of Muḥammad's mission, God raised him to Himself. Muḥammad ﷺ ascended to heaven (*miʿrāj*), and he was made to see the angels, the prophets, Paradise, and Hell. Then, he was brought in the proximity of Allah. When your boss has a trivial message for you,

---

٤ عن أبي ذر رضي الله عنه قال: أوصاني رسول الله عليه السلام بسبع : أوصاني أن أنظر إلى من هودوني ولا أنظر إلى من هو فوقي وأوصاني بحب المساكين والدنو منهم ، وأوصاني أن أقول الحق وإن كان مرا وأوصاني أن أصل رحمي وإن أدبرت ، وأوصاني أن لا أخاف في الله لومة لائم وأوصاني أن أستكثر من قول "لاحول ولا قوه إلا بالله العلي العظيم" "فانها من كنوز الجنة

they may send you an email or give you a call. But when your boss has something very important to say, they will call you into their office to speak to you. God revealed the obligations of charity (zakāt), fasting (sawm), and the Hajj pilgrimage while the Prophet was on Earth. But He revealed the details of prayer (salāt) at the miʿrāj. Allah brought the Prophet to Himself to dictate the number of units each prayer would be. This may be due to the significance of prayer. Prayer is inescapable – one can be exempt from charity if they are poor, exempt from fasting if they are ill, and exempt from pilgrimage if they are unable to go. But if one cannot find water to pray, one uses dust. If he cannot stand, he sits, and if he cannot sit, he lies down and prays. While many of us today neglect prayer, it is the pillar of Islam that is expressed several

times per day. It was the advice of our Messenger ﷺ on his deathbed, and it will be a test for most of us in the Hereafter. Salāt brings the pillars of Islam together into one ritual: in prayer, you recite your testimony of faith (shahāda), you fast from food and drink during prayer, you give charity of your time, and you make your intentions for Mecca.

Unlike the ascensions of other prophets, Muḥammad ﷺ returned to Earth. After recognizing the higher realities, he came back with the perspective of the cosmos to bring order into daily life.

Muḥammad ﷺ called to the way of God to his family and his companions. Many accepted his message, and many rejected it. His enemies called him a sorcerer and a lunatic,

while his followers believed him to be God's Final
Messenger and the fulfillment of many prophecies. He
was peaceful and nonviolent, and in return, his opponents
persecuted him and his followers. They tried to humiliate
him by calling him names, throwing filth at him while he
prayed, and putting thorny obstacles in his path. He only
responded with kindness. As Muḥammad's popularity
grew, his enemies became more and more oppressive.
They began beating Muslims, boycotting their businesses,
and eventually, killing them. When his disciples Yāsir and
Sumayya were publicly tortured to death due to their
faith, it became clear that the Prophet and the Muslims
were no longer welcome in Mecca.

Muḥammad ﷺ had to bear the loss of his dear wife,
Khadīja, and his protecting uncle, Abu Ṭālib, within the
same year. He was also attacked at Ṭā'if, where he bled
from head to toe. He did not raise a finger against his
opponents. Rather, he prayed that their descendants
would eventually accept Islam. After forbearing so much
hardship, an opportunity arose: the people of the city of

Yathrib invited Muḥammad ﷺ to establish a government
there. Yathrib was experiencing a civil dispute, and

Muḥammad ﷺ was the only one who was able to bring
peace and order to the warring tribes there. So, he and his
followers migrated to Yathrib (now known as "Medina")
while the pagans tried to assassinate him.

When the Muslims left their belongings and loved ones in
Mecca, and Allah revealed the accounts of the prophets in
Medina, Allah was not just telling stories to these people

who lost everything. Every story in the Quran is reflected and fulfilled in the life of Prophet Muḥammad ﷺ, his family and his companions. Just as Noah was rescued from the Flood, Abraham was rescued from the fire, Moses was rescued from the Pharaoh, and Jesus was rescued from the cross, Muḥammad ﷺ would be rescued from his enemies. Allah selected the stories of 25 prophets in the Quran out of many thousands, because their lives were a motif that our Messenger ﷺ would fulfill directly.

In Medina, the Muslims wrote a constitution with the locals and established a state. All groups were protected, and the rule of law was put in place. But that was not the end of dismay. Medina was near the Meccan trade route to Syria, and Islam threatened the business of the pagans. The Meccans were looking to quash Islam by any means necessary, because if the Kaʿba were to return to a temple dedicated to the worship of the One God, the Meccans feared that they would fail to attract pagan Arab pilgrims. Islam was also threatening tribal hierarchy by uniting people under God and His Messenger. The Meccans also feared that the rise of Islam would catch the attention of the Romans and the Persians, who presumably had the power to crush any newly-established power in the Arabian peninsula.

The Meccans sent armies to kill Muḥammad ﷺ and his followers, who took up the sword to fight back. Despite their small numbers, lack of equipment, and few horses and camels, the Muslims came out victorious at Badr. At Uhud, the Muslims faced heavy casualties, because many were more concerned with war booty rather than following Muḥammad's orders. At Khandaq, the Muslims successfully defended Medina by digging a trench around the city that prevented the opposing armies from entering.

The cousin and son-in-law of the Prophet was ʿAlī b. Abī Ṭālib. He said, "When the battle intensified on the day of Badr, we sought protection by the Messenger of Allah ﷺ. He was braver than any person that came before. No one would be closer to the pagans [in battle] than him."[5]

Muḥammad's life as a Prophet was simple. He lived in a small mud house, he patched his own clothes, repaired his own shoes, milked his own animals, ate dates and drank milk. He was quiet, humble, and always smiling. He was pleasant and merciful to all people, and he always made sure that everyone's rights were established, and the needs of the people were met. He spent his days and nights praying and fasting. He built alliances between tribes and united all his followers under one Nation.

The Messenger ﷺ was both a man of strength, bravery, and sacred knighthood on one side, and a man of devotional prayer, peace of mind, and tenderness on the other. Men often find it difficult to strike the right balance between the lion and the monk within them. But with

---

5 ـ علي قال: لـما حضر البأس يوم بدر اتقينا برسول الله صلى الله عليه ـ وسلم وكان من أشد الناس ما كان أو لم يكن أحد أقرب إلى المشركين منه.

him ﷺ as your compass, you will know when you have gone too far or have lagged behind.

He was ridiculed, attacked physically, forced out of his hometown, and endured many hardships throughout his life. His loyal family members and companions were killed in the hundreds in order to establish Islam.

As time went by, more and more people were accepting Islam. Finally, in 630 CE, the Prophet and 10,000 Muslims marched to Mecca. The idols of the Kaʿba were destroyed and the temple was restored to its original purpose: the worship of the One God. Muḥammad ﷺ forgave all his opponents, and within a few months, all of them had converted to Islam. By the end of his life, all the Arabs, as well as some Africans, Persians, and Romans, had converted to Islam.

Fourteen hundred years later, the Prophet Muḥammad ﷺ is still relevant. "Muḥammad" is the most popular name in the world. Islam is the fastest growing religion in the world, and the second largest religion in the world. It will soon be the largest religion, by the permission of God.

The Prophet ﷺ was a social reformer, a judge, a diplomat, a military leader, a father, a husband, and a Messenger of Allah. He displayed forbearance, kindness, bravery, mercy, and patience. He was the Servant of God, the Proof of God on the Earth, a Mercy to the Worlds, and the best of mankind. Muslims continue to look to Muḥammad's example - his character, his words, and his actions – as they try to emulate him in their daily lives.

Whenever a Muslim mentions the blessed name of Muḥammad, he asks God to bless him. This is called *ṣalawāt*. *Salawāt* comes from the Arabic word *ṣalāt*. *Ṣalāt* in Arabic literally means "connection." Every time you invoke the *ṣalawāt* on the Messenger, you are asking Allah to further strengthen His connection to the Messenger. Every time you bless the Messenger, you also bless yourself, and strengthen your connection to God. One of God's names is Peace (*as-Salām*). Nobody connects to Peace without also receiving the serenity of God. Thus, if you ever feel conflicted, worried and anxious, increase your *ṣalawāt*.

The Messenger of Allah ﷺ said, "None of you truly believes until I am more beloved to him than his child, his father and all the people."[6]

One may ask, how can we voluntarily love someone? Love is, at least partly, involuntary – you can't explain how or why you love someone; you just do. "God does not burden any soul with more than it can bear" (2:286) This is possible because Allah embedded characteristics in the Prophet ﷺ that are universally beautiful. Those who learn about his life with an open heart cannot help but fall hopelessly in love with him. It is when you gain knowledge that you realize the nobility that is inherent to him.

We may not see the Prophet in this world, but the true believers emulate him as closely as possible. They say his

---

⁶ لاَ يُؤْمِنُ أَحَدُكُمْ حَتَّى أَكُونَ أَحَبَّ إِلَيْهِ مِنْ وَلَدِهِ وَوَالِدِهِ وَالنَّاسِ أَجْمَعِينَ

words, they perfume themselves in his fragrance, they eat what he ate, they wear what he wore, they establish justice, they forebear trials, and devote themselves in worship. No believer will attain the excellence of the Prophet, but they may attain a slight whiff of one or two of his characteristics. Thus, the archetype of the Prophet is present in the amalgamation of a company of believers. After all, the Prophet lived in accordance to the natural telos (*fiṭra*), and the *fiṭra* is in each one of us.

The scent of musk is a timeless, spaceless connection that we have to the Prophet ﷺ. We may not be able to see his face or hear his voice in this world, but we often neglect olfaction, which could give us a "whiff" of his presence.

It is reported that Anas said, "I have never smelt musk nor ambergris that was sweeter than his fragrance."[7]

But not only does this fragrance bring us to him – it gives us a sense of Paradise. Perfume is the soil of Paradise. The Prophet ﷺ said, "Its soil is white, shining, pure musk" (دَرْمَكَةٌ بَيْضَاءُ مِسْكٌ خَالِصٌ), and like him, even "sweeter than musk" (أَطْيَبُ مِنَ الْمِسْكِ). In some narrations in Ṭabari, it is said that perfume came down from heaven with Adam and Eve and clung to the plants thereafter. The Messenger loved perfume because it was the scent of his true home. So, if you miss the man, embody his Sunna.

وَلاَ عَنْبَرَةً أَطْيَبَ مِنْ رَائِحَةِ رَسُولِ اللَّهِ صلى الله عليه وسلم . [7]

God says in the Quran, "It is He who sent His Messenger with guidance and the religion of truth to manifest it over all religion, even if the pagans may be averse." (61:9)

This verse applies both on a macrocosmic and microcosmic level. On the macrocosmic level, Islam will supersede all ways of life, because that is the nature of truth. Falsehood does not stand the test of time (17:81) – reality always wins, even if after a while. As the Latin saying goes, "You can drive nature out with a pitchfork, but she'll constantly be rushing back" (*naturam expellas furca tamen usque recurret.*)

On the microcosmic level, the Prophet Muḥammad ﷺ was the embodiment of Islam, and the realization of its fullest potential. Hence, he superseded all people in human history. He was named "the most influential person in history" in Michael Hart's book, because he reached the epitome of religious and personal success. He is perhaps the most written about person in human history and will soon be the man with the greatest number of adherents.

All the pagans that opposed Muḥammad ﷺ were manifestations of their own false religions and idols, and thus they failed and vanished. So, will you be an exponent of the victorious or the dead?

If you would like to revive traditional prophetic ethics, then:

Keep a strong, slim, healthy body.

Clean your teeth often.

Walk swiftly towards your destination.

Do not stare – keep a humble glance and lower your gaze.

Do not speak unless it is necessary.

Keep your words straight to the point, and being conscious of how long you have been speaking.

Avoid vulgar talk.

Immerse yourself in contemplation.

Give importance to the speech and opinion of others.

Never blame people, omen, or nature.

Avoid obsessing over the taste of a food (good or bad).

Be active in fulfilling the rights of others. Act against injustices, small and large.

Limit your laughter to a smile.

Only enter a place from its entrance, and leave it from its exit.

Spend time with God, your family, and your self.

Fulfill the needs of the people and make them happy.

Ask people about their health and their needs.

Greet the leaders of the people and treat them with their due nobility.

Remember God in all meetings, and when you stand and when you sit.

Treat and honour all people equally in your meetings. Do not pick favourites.

Smile, be cheerful, and have a good temper.

Avoid pointing at people with your finger. Instead, point at them with your entire hand.

Have long, endearing handshakes.

Be patient, shy, honest, and trustworthy.
If someone asks for a favour, reply gently and return them with more than what they asked for.

Do not be stern, do not yell, do not be harsh, and do not swear.

Do not point out the faults of others.

Do not interrupt anyone.

Avoid saying 'if only [such and such took place]' and

accept fate.

Turn your body and face towards whomever you are talking to.

Picture yourself in the middle of a desert. It is rough, dry, and dusty. The Sun burns your skin, and the cloudless sky produces no shade. It is almost barren, and there is very little life. All of a sudden, you find a date palm with fresh dates on it. The dates are sweet, juicy, and nourishing. You are amazed that something so delightful and so healthy could grow in such an arid place. It is the same with our Prophet. Like the desert, Jāhilīyya was a barren place with dead hearts. The environment was hostile   a place empty of prophets and revelation, and full of ignorance and barbarism. Yet the Prophet was a sweet, shy, beautiful man who brought us the life of faith; nourishment to our souls. It is reported that the Prophet

Muḥammad ﷺ said, "If a fresh date comes, then commend me; and if it goes, then console me."[8]

A sweet, nourishing gift from an arid, vacuous, hostile

land — the Prophet Muḥammad ﷺ.

---

[8] وقال صلى الله عليه وآله وسلم: إذا جاء الرطب فهنئوني ، وإذا ذهب فعزوني

32

Chapter 3

Oakmoss: Gnosis of the Divine

***

Oakmoss has a strong, earthy-mossy aroma. It is like the wet forest ground, and it is very true to nature. If revelation is like rain (16:64), and water is the foundation of life (21:30), then oakmoss is a suitable metaphor for sacred knowledge.

The base identity of every person is that he or she is a creation and servant of God. That is why we are all called Abdullāh and Amatullāh – that is who we fundamentally are.

Regardless of one's sex, race, or even religious beliefs, all humans are created to manifest the glory of God. The Quran and *ḥadīth* often refer to all human beings as *'ibād* (servants), all of whom ultimately abide by His will (30:26). Humans have been given a will, and with that will, a human can either reach his natural telos by developing his intellect, mastering language, and representing God; or by giving into ignorance and base appetites. In this sense, man is both celestial and earthly; spiritual and natural.

All humans have a common, meek, worldly state, but the goal is to humbly ascend back to God. We are all from Adam and Adam is from dust; but we belong to Allah and to Him we will return.

"Whoso knows his self, assuredly knows his Lord." The prophets, messengers, and *awliya'* had a self-awareness, believing that their selves were a part of a grander creation, whose origin and point of return is Allah. This is an expression of the weak, limitedness of man, which thus highlights the strength and capacity of Allah. This means that one must acknowledge the most fundamental and essential fact about himself: that he was created, and therefore, he is a finite, needing a Creator and Sustainer. One must realize the constraints of his own power and his intelligence to understand He who is All-Powerful and All-Knowing. That is the beginning of the process of gnosis (*ma'rifa*) where one surrenders himself in faith and in action to Absolute Perfection.

We bear witness that Muḥammad is Allah's Servant and His Messenger, which is an acknowledgement of the primacy of the servitude of Muḥammad ﷺ to his Lord. This servitude is the key to true greatness, because one who is a slave to God cannot be a slave to worldliness. All people surrender, whether to their own desires or to an outside force, but if one's reliance is completely on Allah, he will be free from obeying others. One who fears only Allah does not fear anything else, which elevates his status in the creation. It is the Prophet Muḥammad's sincere service to Allah that made him the best of creation.

Identifying yourself with what you eat or who you have sex with is very shallow. Food and sex are functions of the lower self. Identifying with a race is identifying with an accidental characteristic of yourself rather than your essential nature. As much as these "tribes" may be relevant in today's world, we should not be fixated on *ʿasabiyya* (tribalism, group mentality), which was the underlining feature of Jāhilīyya. Identity politics can blind us from ethics, which should be rooted more in verbs and adverbs than in nouns and pronouns. It can cause irreparable division and segregation. It can cause us to lose focus of our purpose and goal: "And I did not create the jinn and mankind except to worship Me." (51:56) Know yourself, and then you will begin to know Allah.

Maʿrifa means recognition, cognizance and gnosis. It is the Arabic opposite of Jāhilīyya. Messenger Muḥammad ﷺ fought against Jāhilīyya for his whole life. *Jahl* is ignorance, foolhardiness, stupidity, pretending to know nothing, and closing one's eyes to the truth. Its heedlessness confusion blinded people from God and the Last Day. The climax of his mission was his Farewell Hajj.

35

The entire ritual of Hajj is predicated on sacrificing oneself to God. The shaven heads, the wearing of garments resembling burial shrouds, the commemoration of Abraham and Ishmael, and the final sacrifice of the animal: these are all important symbols that we belong fully to God, and that our lives are in His hand. The animal sacrifice is called a *qurbān*, because it is sacrifice that brings us nearer (*qurb*) to God. At the end of Hajj, you come out sinless, which is your rebirth after your sacrifice. And all of this can be summarized into one word – Islam – complete and full submission to God's will.

The climax of Hajj is the Day of *'Arafa*, from the same root as *ma'rifa*. It is the day where one is to realize his purpose. The servant opens his eyes to see the temporal nature of this world and sets his heart on the next world. The Day of *'Arafa* is when you are to expunge all ignorance from your self, on the individual and collective level. The Day of *'Arafa* is when the Messenger put everything on the table in his Farewell Sermon. He said, "I left you on a clear plain: its night is like its day, and none deviates from it except that he perishes."[9] Gnosis requires clarity.

It is on Mount *'Arafa* that the Messenger delivered his most comprehensive message to the largest audience he would ever address in his worldly life. It is here that the Messenger left behind his Two Weighty Things, the *Thaqalayn* – and all Muslims should seek gnosis of them.

---

9 تركتكم على المحجة البيضاء ليلها كنهارها لا يزيغ عنها إلا هالك

This world is a perpetual war between Intellect (*'aql*) and Ignorance (*jahl*). This is reflected both inwardly and outwardly. The epitome of outward *jahl* is Jāhilīyya, and the epitome of inward *jahl* is a hard heart. Hard-heartedness is the root of all evil, because the outward is the exponent of the inward.

The core of the Jāhilīyya society was the Kāʿba, but it was a Kāʿba that was filled with idols and surrounded by animalistic nakedness. To cleanse Mecca, which is the epicentre of the Earth, the Messenger ﷺ had to begin by cleansing the Kāʿba of its idols. Similarly, *tawḥīd* is the process of monotheizing by expunging the idols of one's heart.

The leaders of Jāhilīyya are called "the Imams of Disbelief" (*a'immat al-kufr*) in the Quran, among whom was Abu Jahl, "the Father of Ignorance."

In the story of Moses, Moses represented the intellect and its forces, including knowledge and humility; whilst Pharaoh represented ignorance and its forces, including greed and arrogance. In the example of Ḥusayn, ignorance resurged in the person of Yazīd, who although held the title of caliph, was a ruthless, lustful, foolish drunk. This is a lesson that even the holy pulpit can be ascended by apes. Both Moses and Ḥusayn attained victory, but in different directions. Their *'aql* conquered *jahl*, even if their physical outcomes were different. The selfless struggle of Moses against Pharaoh and the struggle of Husayn can be summarized in one word – Islam.

In the Hereafter, Allah will annihilate ignorance, as falsehood by its nature is a perishing thing (17:81). There will be no Hegelian synthesis of intellect and ignorance – the intellect will win completely and absolutely when its time is fulfilled. Any victories that ignorance may have in this world are only apparent and temporary.

Most are satisfied with their level of intellect, but they're not satisfied with their sustenance (*rizq*). In reality, we should be satisfied with our sustenance, and not satisfied with our level of intellect – and always vying to improve. Some people have great theoretical knowledge but are lazy in their worship. Others are committed and disciplined in their worship but remain ignorant. It's very rare to find someone who has mastered the best of both. But your worship should lead you to intellectual curiosity, and your knowledge should lead you to good works.

Intellect should not be confused with mere logic. Our logic is not the same as Allah's knowledge. Putting your baby in the Nile River seems like a horrific idea. Having that child raised by a tyrannical Pharaoh may be even worse. But that was the order of Allah, and His ways are not ours. We can try our best to be objective, but without access to all information, and with emotional variables and intellectual boundaries, much of our reasoning is guesswork. Many people have knowledge, but wisdom is applying the right knowledge at the right time in the right place. You must look 40 generations ahead of you and 40 generations behind you. Find what is timeless and become timeless yourself.

The Quran creates a hierarchy of applied gnosis. The Quran says that those who know are not equal to those who do not know (39:9). Adam's authority was demonstrated through his knowledge of the names, which the angels did not have (2:30-34). Saul's authority was also based on his intellect (2:247). The Hereafter itself is a hierarchy of ethics. Human societies thus need to define competence in light of knowledge by rewarding those who act on sound uses of their intellect.

Knowledge is power. Allah recounts a relevant parable in the Quran: "But one who had knowledge of the Book said, 'I can bring it to you in the twinkling of an eye.'" (27:40) In this verse, it is reported that 'Asif b. Barkhīyya transported the throne of the Queen of Sheba to Solomon's court using religious knowledge (*'ilmun min al-kitāb*). He was able to bring it faster even than the jinn in the previous verse, despite being human. Hence, if Islamic knowledge is understood and practiced correctly, it can be even more powerful than paranormal forces – let alone an army, state, or market.

Likewise, when al-Khidr rebuilt the wall in Surat al-Kahf, the wall was hiding the inheritance of orphans. The Quran describes this inheritance as a treasure (كنز) that belonged to a righteous man. The wall was falling apart, so al-Khidr fixed it, in a village of undeserving people. Many authorities report that this treasure was a tablet made of gold. Written on it was the following: "In the name of Allah, the Beneficent, the Merciful. I am astonished at he who believes in destiny: how does he become sorrowful? I am astonished at he who believes in death: how does he become happy? And I am astonished at he who recognizes this world, and how it is volatile with its people: how does he put his trust in it? There is no god except Allah, and Muḥammad is the Messenger of Allah."[10]

There is no greater inheritance than the truth. Make sure you leave this world not just with no debts, but with a legacy of wisdom. Al-Khidr showed us that wisdom is worth saving – and Allah knows best.

So, could sacred knowledge alone change the world? If you took your smartphone back in time, to the Middle Ages, it would get two types of reactions. The first group of people would be dazzled by it and be thankful for its utility. They could use it to learn how to better their lives. The second group would see you as a threat. You and your fancy device could change the power structure and uncover their benevolent lies. They will try to kill you, and either break your phone or co-opt your phone to continue to exploit others. This is how the prophets were. They came to their communities with an otherworldly intellect, signs, and a message. There were those who were amazed, thankful, and used the message to better their lives. And, there were those who were afraid of losing their leadership, their riches, and their mythologies. So, they covered the truth (*kufr*) and tried to kill the prophets. When the message was already out, they tried

---

10 بسم الله الرحمن الرحيم ، عجبت لمن يؤمن بالقدر كيف يحزن؟ وعجبت لمن يوقن بالموت كيف يفرح؟ وعجبت لمن يعرف الدنيا وتقلبها بأهلها كيف يطمئن إليها؟ لا إله إلا الله ، محمد رسول الله

to destroy the message, or to co-opt (*nifāq*) it for their exploitative usages.

Thus, the prophets were not just deliverers of sacred knowledge. They also could not have just demanded that people accept their knowledge. The Messenger ﷺ could not have just shown up to Jāhilīyya and said, "the Quran says this, so we have to do it." He had to establish his authority by persuading those with open hearts. He used his good manners, rational arguments, his noble reputation, and miracles to bring people into faith. Then, once faith was established, listening and obeying was incumbent upon them. The Quran utilizes arguments from nature, the law of non-contradiction, historical precedents, and rational arguments against polytheists and trinitarians to convince its audience.

Whilst the basis of the *shahāda* is logic, the Messenger ﷺ did not rely exclusively on logic. If you read the conversion stories of the companions, most of them became Muslim due to his character. This is because intuition (*fiṭra*) goes beyond reason. Most theists don't know the cosmological and ontological arguments for God, yet they still believe in God, because they simply know Him by nature. Even in post-Christian America, while organized religion is on the decline, the vast majority of people still hold onto the belief in a Higher Power. There is nothing shameful about those who believe out of intuition. The faith of a village grandmother may be more valuable than that of an armchair keyboard warrior with seventy arguments for God's existence.

God is not only experienced in our sacred books, but also in sanctified people, in solitude, in the beauty of nature, in aesthetics, and in silence. Allah could have created just our souls, but He housed us in a marvelous universe, all of which is a theatre of His majesty. The world itself is a theophany and a revelation. The Messenger himself ﷺ is the best example of God's justice and grace. Meditating on his example will bring one closer to *ma'rifa*.

With God's permission, Muḥammad ﷺ gave sight to those blinded by polytheism. He gave hearing to those who had never heard the scripture. He made the dumb speak with wisdom and eloquence. He made the lame walk and overcome the civilizations of the Earth. And, he raised the spiritually dead to the life of faith. Muḥammad ﷺ was on the *fiṭra*, and the *fiṭra* is in you. So be Muḥammadi.

Praxis is the outward component of gnosis. The first crucial step to changing the world is changing yourself – that is the only way that Allah will change our social conditions (13:11). Mastering the *nafs* is thus the basis of Islam. The *nafs* is basically a term that refers to the appetitive nature of human. It can be compared to Plato's "many-headed beast", or Freud's "ego", or also the New Age "lower self". It is the desirous and selfish part of man, the part of you that desires physical and mental satiation.

Every person has a *nafs*. If a person's *nafs* overpowers their intellect, then they are animalistic, because they

42

think with their stomach, their private, etc. If a person's intellect overpowers their *nafs*, then they are balanced and healthy, because they only feed their *nafs* with what is appropriate. We all must feed the *nafs* – we all need to eat, we all need to marry, we all need some form of validation – but we should seek those things within the *ḥalāl*, and in moderation.

Once we have mastered our *nafs*, we will be one step closer to understanding "reality". The words "reality" and "*ḥaqīqa*" (حقيقة) are often used interchangeably, but their subtle etymological differences reflect an important worldview difference. The root of "reality" is the Latin word "res", which means "thing". The root of *ḥaqīqa* is *ḥaq* (حق), which means "truth". The Truth, *al-Ḥaq*, is Allah. He is the ultimate truth behind all truths, which means that we must look for Him in every sign we see. A mere understanding of "things" however will not arrive at meaning. The Quran says, "They know what is apparent of the worldly life, but they, of the Hereafter, are unaware." (30:7) One may have a thorough understanding of tangible "things" – the natural sciences – but no understanding of *ḥaqīqa*.

"Faith, without works, is dead." (James 2:26) Good deeds are the outward quality of faith. Faith, when strong enough, will cause you to do good and abstain from evil. If you believe that fire is hot, and that it will harm you, and that there is no goodness in this harm, then you'll avoid touching it. Likewise, if you truly know God and make Him your focal point (*taqwa*), then you'll behave as though He is always watching you.

We all struggle with certain sins – that is because we don't fully comprehend the consequences of those sins. If I told you to eat a rotting piece of meat on the side of the road, you'll tell me that I'm mad. That meat would taste awful and cause you illness. That is the nature of sin: in this world, it is just a fleeting and disturbing thing; and in the next world, it is pain and destruction. It is heedlessness of God and neglect of the Hereafter that causes us to sin. Hence, while we are sinning, the light of faith leaves our heart.

Faith is a conscience that makes you return to reason once you have done something wrong. It makes you want to undo the damage that you have brought about. It will cause you to find a bandage for your burn, or a medicine for your illness; which in the spiritual world is repentance, penance, atonement, self-awareness, and the performance of good works. Sin is misguided and stupid of us, but to turn back to God and to reform our ways is a thing of beauty. Had we never sinned, God would have replaced us with a species that did sin, just so that He could forgive them after sincere repentance.

Faith, without works, is dead. The devil knows that there is a God and a Hereafter, but he does not act on that knowledge, and thus he has no faith. That is the worst form of evil – knowing something is wrong, then doing it anyway, without fear of its consequences. This type of evil is temporary in the creation, and Allah will bring it to an end in the Hereafter. And, in the end, none of us will go to Paradise except by divine grace – *raḥma*.

We may not be able to fully understand God, but we know Him. To give a parallel example: you may not be able to describe your love with mere words. Once you can explain love, it ceases to be love. Love is better known than explained. God is not known by the senses, but rather His reality is recognized and acknowledged by the heart. It is reported that Zayn al-'Abidīn said, "My God! Tongues fall short of praising You in a way that fits Your majesty. Intellects fail at grasping the core of Your beauty. Eyes fail before gazing upon the glories of Your face. You have assigned to Your creatures no way to know You, except in their incapacity to know You!"[11]

In truth,
there is no ornament, no embellishment,
no decoration, no illumination,
no being, no meaning,
no order from disorder,
no remedy from malady,
no salvation from damnation,
no relief from grief,
like Belief.

١١ إِلٰهِي قَصُرَتِ الْأَلْسُنُ عَنْ بُلُوغِ ثَنائِكَ، كَما يَلِيقُ بِجَلالِكَ،
وَعَجَزَتِ الْعُقُولُ عَنْ إِدْراكِ كُنْهِ جَمالِكَ،
وَانْحَسَرَتِ الْأَبْصارُ دُونَ النَّظَرِ إِلىٰ سُبُحاتِ وَجْهِكَ،
وَلَمْ تَجْعَلْ لِلْخَلْقِ طَرِيقاً إِلىٰ مَعْرِفَتِكَ
إِلّاَ بِالْعَجْزِ عَنْ مَعْرِفَتِكَ

Chapter 4

Patchouli: Finding Beauty in Suffering

* * *

Patchouli is a strong, sweet, intoxicating scent. It has a dark, earthy aroma, yet it is musky. It is a rather unusual contradiction, yet it is a fragrant that dominates our senses.

Likewise, love and suffering are a match made in heaven.

Love is breathlessly heart-wrenching, as it snares the mind of the lover and controls his actions. Any loving relationship will be filled with trial and tribulation, selfless sacrifice, selfish protectiveness, and frequent heartbreak.

We both live and die for even a moment of true love.

It is thus no coincidence that suffering is a component of many Arabic words for love. *Ishq* (عشق), which is a fervent type of love, was originally a vine that winds itself around a tree, squeezing it until it withered. *Shaghaf* (شغف), which is passion, was a form of heart disease. *Muhjata qalb* (مهجة قلب), an expression used to describe a lover, is actually the blood of the heart. *Huyūm* (الهيوم), meaning passion, is a type of insanity. The Persian poem of Layla and Majnūn comes to mind.

With that in mind, reanalyze the Quranic accounts. Abraham was ordered to sacrifice his own firstborn son. Moses' mother loved him, but she had to put him into the Nile River. Jacob wept over his favourite son Joseph until he went blind. Zulaykha had passion (*shaghaf*) for Joseph (12:3), but it led to his imprisonment and her humiliation. A woman is compared to a farm in 2:223, because a man must put in labour to bear her fruits.

There are a few lessons here. Firstly: love is a verb, and it requires effort, and often, the lover pays a valuable price. So, make Allah your number one love, and seek His satisfaction at the behest of this world.

Second: there isn't really a concept of "happily ever after" in this world. It is rather seen as a prison of the believer, an abode of trials (*dār al-balā '*), and a fleeting world (*dār al-fanā '*). As the Prophet ﷺ famously said, "Those who

47

suffer the most are the prophets, then those similar to them, then those similar those similar to them."[12]

Third: suffering is redemptive. It has a spiritual function in this world: it can remove our sins, it can give us humility and character, and it can be our chastisement. To remove all suffering from this life is not possible, and not necessarily desirable either. It refines us and helps us grow.

Fourth: love is not everything. An infatuation can seem paradisal, but go back to the story of Joseph. He had what most of us desire: a perfect appearance, a noble family, and the love of others. But that only led to the jealousy of his brothers, the plotting of desirous women, and his imprisonment. What brought him up from that lowest part of his life was KNOWLEDGE, and from there, he became a ruler in his land and reconciled with his family.

Love is the intense vigilance that a mother has over her child, the undying loyalty that a person has for their spouse, and the forsaken mourning of a widow. It is a bond closer than family and thicker than blood. May Allah allow us to love as He would love us to. "Say: 'If you love God, then follow me, and God will love you, and forgive you your sins; God is the Forgiving, the Compassionate.'" (3:31)

إن من أشد الناس بلاء الأنبياء ، ثم الذين يلونهم ، ثم الذين يلونهم [12]

While suffering is not a linear indicator of righteousness, the righteous will endure more trials than others, because ethics is not mere pragmatism. Righteousness will occasionally cost you. This world, this prison, is a purgatory that prepares the righteous for meeting with God.

The way we conceptualize suffering is influenced by neurological factors, as well as cultural and educational factors. Hence, a "no pain, no gain" approach to suffering may constructively expand the self rather than attack or destroy it.

This is not meant to be masochistic or sadistic in any way: suffering is not to be glorified, rather the Islamic tradition takes many steps to restrict it; but the logical end of upholding an ideal is being accountable to it, even if it means that one must take a loss. While some ideologues gloat their victimhood to a pathological degree, the Muslim is commonly encouraged to look at his problems as a storm in a teacup.

When we experience pain, just remember the pain of the Beloved Prophet ﷺ and his family, who suffered the most despite being the best of people. Your pain is not a deity that is to be feared or worshiped – we are to forebear it with steadfastness and patience.

The life of Muḥammad ﷺ, his family and their devoted companions and students taught me that:

love is paired with *suffering,*
intelligence is paired with *humility,*
words are paired with *beauty,*
justice is paired with *mercy,*
hardship is paired with *purification,*
and that *hope* is paired with *fear.*

They are forever married to one another, until death parts them.

Revenge for many people is a bigger virtue than forgiveness, but there is no dignity in revenge. The Messenger of Allah ﷺ forgave and guided his opponents after his march on Mecca. This was after they displaced him and killed many of his relatives and followers. Victimization blinds one from the suffering of others. It makes us bitter, not better. It hardens our hearts. It makes us only see power and deal only in power transactions. It justifies revenge and disproportionate responses.

Our Messenger ﷺ would never say "if only..." (لو). He knew that circumstances would not always go according to plan. He lost his parents, his grandfather, his wife, his uncles, his homeland... but he smiled. He forgave his opponents. He clung to patience and prayer. He restrained his anger. And eventually, his character won over his hardened enemies.

Imagine if the prophets of God had developed a victim complex. They would have only focused on how the world wronged them, rather than empathizing with the oppression of others. They would have expected the worst in people, and not make excuses for anyone (*sū'ath-thann*). They would have been rampant with negative emotions, rather than smiling at everyone that they met. They would have believed that they were powerless to bring about change, rather than trying to change and civilize their people. They would have been pessimists, rather than having hope in God. They would have blamed all of their problems on others, rather than employing a sense of responsibility and accountability. They would indulge in self-pity, rather than directing that mercy towards others. They would have been passive-aggressive, rather than assertive yet understanding. They would have set themselves up for utter failure.

Our Umma faces many immense challenges today, but the miracle of Islam is that the Prophet ﷺ was able to come an Ignorant people, and awaken those who were spiritually dead, give hearing to the spiritually deaf, give sight to the spiritually blind, make the spiritually lame walk, and make his neglected community into a world civilization. Muḥammad ﷺ lost family members, he lost his home, he bled from head-to-toe, he suffered poverty, and he had armies trying to kill him. Yet, he shone forth like the full moon. He pardoned his enemies, who were touched not just by his message, but by his grace.

The toughest decision that a victim can make is to forgive one who transgresses him. Being the recipient of harm is demanding on one's spirit. But revenge is only "getting even" with your persecutor, and two wrongs do not make a right. What truly raises you is forgiveness. Forgiveness releases some of your pain and brings benevolence into the world. After being wronged by his brothers, Joseph said to them, "No blame will there be upon you today. Allah will forgive you; and He is the Most Merciful of the merciful." (12:92)

Socrates said when he was being tried to death, "No evil can happen to a good man, either in life or after death." Lady Zaynab said to the tyrant Yazid after the greatest tragedy in the Islamic chronicle: "I saw nothing but beauty."[13] The "Contented Soul" of the Quran is content with Allah's decree, and not blaming or blameworthy.

Jāʿfar as-Sādiq, the great-grandson of the Prophet ﷺ, said, "I am amazed by the Muslim man, Allah does not decree for him but that it be good for him. If he were cut by scissors, it would be good for him; and if he owned the East and the West, it would be good for him."[14]

Every problem is an opportunity in disguise. Do not catastrophize. Healing begins when you shed victimhood for good and bring the beauty that forbearance has taught you into the world.

---

13 ما رأيت الا جميلاً
14 عجبت للمرء المسلم لا يقضي الله عز وجل له قضاء إلا كان خيرا له،
إن قرض بالمقاريض كان خيرا له، وإن ملك مشارق الارض ومغاربها
كان خيرا له.

Chapter 5

Lavender: A Deep Breath for Mental Health

✳✳✳

The Messenger of Allah ﷺ passed by a group of people who were gathered. He asked them, "What have you gathered here for?" They said, "O Messenger of Allah! This person is an insane epileptic, so we gathered around him." So the Messenger ﷺ said, "He is not insane, but rather, he is being tried. Shall I not tell you who is truly insane?" They said, "Of course, O Messenger of Allah!" He

ﷺ said, "The one who is truly insane is he who walks with pride, who only looks at people from the corner of his eye, who struts with his shoulders, who wishes for Allah's Paradise yet disobeys him; one from whose evil there is no protection, nor is there hope that he would do good – such a person is insane. This person however is just being tried."[15]

Fitna in Arabic literally means a fire that refines gold. That means that every sedition, trial, tribulation, and temptation can have two outcomes. It can either destroy and disintegrate you, or it can purify and strengthen you. For gold to become gold, it must first be put into the fire. That fire will remove all its excess minerals, until it becomes pure. Allah says in the Quran, "Do the people think that they will be left to say, 'We believe' and they will not be tried? (*yuftanūn*)? But We have certainly tried those before them, and Allah will surely make evident those who are truthful, and He will surely make evident the liars." (29:2-3)

Anxiety is a constant feeling of drowning. You choke on nothing, and you can't breathe. Your chest tightens, your heart rate rapidly increases, your arms and feet get numb,

---

15 مر رسول الله صلى الله عليه وآله على جماعة فقال: على ما اجتمعتم؟ قالوا: يارسول الله هذا مجنون يصرع، فاجتمعنا عليه،فقال: ليس هذا بمجنون ولكنه المبتلى، ثم قال: ألا اخبركم بالمجنون حق المجنون؟ قالوا: بلى يارسول الله قال: [إن المجنون حق المجنون المتبختر في مشيته، الناظر في عطفيه، المحرك جنبيه بمنكبيه، يتمنى على الله جنته وهو يعصيه، الذي لا يؤمن شره، ولا يرجى خيره، فذلك المجنون، وهذا المبتلى

and your head gets dizzy. Living with anxiety feels like living with death.

The bright side of this is that death is no longer a stranger. The Hereafter becomes clear as day, and the light at the end of the tunnel is always visible and even endearing. You end up seizing the day and focusing on the important things in life. You truly live life like it is temporary and live a sober existence.

Even at the worst moments, pain takes the sins from your body. You become humble to your mortality and sensitive to the illnesses of others. You become better, beautiful even. Part of becoming whole is knowing how much your pain has made you a more patient and forbearing servant of God. We aren't born whole, but the moon teaches us that you do not have to be whole to shine. Part of getting better is knowing that things will never be perfect, and you will never be all-powerful, but you can always make a positive difference in your self and in your surroundings.

Some things are known by their opposites. It takes the existence of evil to truly understand and appreciate good. Without poverty, there could never be charity. Suffering gives us a chance to be good. The Creator can be known by virtue of the existence of the creation. Likewise, our own faults and shortcomings are to humble us to One who has no faults or shortcomings. Our powerlessness only highlights the absolute power of Allah. As the saying goes, "whoever knows himself knows his Lord."

Happiness has never been my goal. Success in life cannot be measured by a simple X-Y graph that plots us on a linear scale of happiness; nor does happiness necessarily exist on a binary level. When we tell people that the goal in life is to be happy, we're simultaneously telling all unhappy people that they have failed in life. But this is not true. Throughout the year, there will be moments where you will feel happy, sad, or any range of simple or complex emotions.

What's more important than happiness is contentment. We want to be at peace, and we pray for God's peace every time we greet one another. Quiet of mind and peace at heart is how we get through sadness with hope and patience. Happiness must be balanced with sobriety. We must pray that Allah makes us *rāḍiyatan marḍiyya* – well-pleased and pleasing to Him.

Abu Zayd al-Balkhī (d. 934) was a scientist who made a distinction between spiritual depression and biological depression. He based his theories on the Quran and Sunna While the medical science of his time focused on physical illnesses, al-Balkhī wrote about spiritual, psychological, and mental disorders. He argued for the interplay between physical and mental health – that bodily illnesses can lead to cognitive problems, and that spiritual illnesses can lead to physical ones. Al-Balkhī wrote about neurosis (chronic distress but without delusions or hallucinations), endogenous depression (originating from within the body), reactive depression (originating from outside the body), and so much that we credit modern psychologists with.

Islam is a religion of faith and actions. While our traditional cultures overemphasize "pray-it-away" solutions to mental health, modern secularism overemphasizes the role of biochemistry. We don't just pray for poverty to go away – we give to charity and we stress personal responsibility and hard work. By the same token, we cannot just throw money at the problem of poverty and expect it to disappear – that can make it even worse.

Clinics and hospitals today are realizing the importance of having chaplains, who are part-in-parcel of the healing process. While medication may lower symptoms and even save lives, there are no "magic pills" – one's worldview, perspective, and lifestyle will bring equal or greater results.

As a Muslim who has struggled with clinical depression, I personally found much of pop psychology and social media "self-care" posts to be narcissistic, anti-social, hedonistic; and perhaps worst of all, they don't work, and could make the problems worse. Some hip shaykhs even erroneously use this playbook. There aren't many Islamic works on the topic, but as we can see from the example of al-Balkhī, the Muslim world developed a foundation to this science over a millennium ago.

Worship, supplication, recitation, *tasbīḥ* and meditation are not necessarily the end-all-be-all solutions to mental health problems. However, we should not denigrate the role of prayer in healing, when in fact prayer has been a source of strength for suffering people. We Muslims even recite prayers upon our physical illnesses, because we know that God is the source of healing, ash-Shāfī, so why not also upon our depressed and our anxious?

As believers in the supernatural, we also believe that envy (ḥasad) and sprites (jinn) can influence our health. Suffering is a spiritual problem as much as it is a physical one, and we have been advised to recite Surat al-Falaq, Surat an-Nās, Surat al-Fātiḥa, and Ayat al-Kursī to remove these maladies.

The promise of future success is always there, especially when we are young and physically healthy, and so one should never feel overwhelmed by the world. If Noah could survive the Flood, if Abraham could make it out of a burning fire, if Moses could make it alive from Pharaoh, if Jesus could overcome the cross, and if Muḥammad ﷺ could become the most successful human to ever live, then we can make it out of our social and financial troubles. That is easy for Allah. Even if we don't, then this world is just a brief break for the traveler.

A good way to fight depression is to train your mind to be solution-oriented rather than problem-oriented. The problem-oriented side is a survival trait and a necessary one, but in the modern day, where imminent physical dangers are few, it's important to not just see the missing tiles, but the tiles that are there. If you find yourself stagnant, not making progress in your life, you must assess what advantages and skills you have. We can wallow in our problems all day – we all live difficult lives – but start counting the things you do have and see what you can do with them.

To be happy is to be grateful. Gratitude is the feeling that you've been given something that you don't deserve;

something that you're lucky to have. One can only be grateful all the time if they are humble. Humility is achieved through knowledge.

Fighting depression is a stressful and tough task, but in the meantime, you could try to make it work for you:

Use your lack of appetite to fast more.
Use your sleep changes to pray at night.
Use your self-criticism to battle your *nafs*.
Use your loss of energy to avoid haram activities.
Consider your aches and pains to be a purification that cleanses you of your sins.
Empathize with the emotional well-being of those around you.

There is a reason for everything, including your maladies. Repurpose your depression, so that it is not purely a negative force, but a force of change.

There will be an inevitable change in your life, but that change will either be brought about by your will or by your circumstances. You must either choose to roll up your sleeves and get to work or wait until the circumstances get more desperate and you are forced to change. It's better for you to choose the time, place and arena than for them to choose you when you're not ready. So much of our stress is a result of us standing in the shadow of our potential self. The duties that we neglect cause us more stress than the duties we fulfill. But if you rise to your responsibilities and give them your all, you'll look and feel healthier.

And there is no power nor force except through Allah, so start all activities with the intention of pleasing Him. Pray for help, and then go help yourself.

What do you do when you are drowning in worries and negative thinking? A fellow wayfarer once shared this important lesson with me: when you experience a downward spiral of negative thoughts or emotions, learn to identify the ego-self from your real self. Then, you can more quickly detect the thoughts that "aren't yours." That way, you can watch your thoughts from the side, rather than spin down with them.

The real self is the silent thinker, based in *fiṭra* and not swayed by reactionary mood swings and narcissistic babble. The ego self is a defense mechanism we build subconsciously to protect our self-importance (self-praise and self-pity).

Allah says in the Quran, "Taha, We have not revealed the Qur'an to you so that you would be distressed." (20:2). The inverse of being distressed or sorrowful (تشقى) in Arabic would be to be glad (تسعد). Revelation is a divine intervention that answers our questions about the nature of the world. The Prophet ﷺ is called a bringer of glad tidings (بشير), because he has come to reassure you that your goodness will not go to waste.

The state of the world is sad – it always has been, it always will be. This world is a purgatory that will constantly try and refine you. Whether we are poor and wretched, or we are living in mansions, we will always be afflicted with pain and sorrow. But this revelation is a source of strength and patience, with which we can keep pushing forward.

Gratitude is the ultimate rebellion against postmodernism. Being resentful is easy, but it is destructive. Focusing on what is missing in your life will lead you to bitter pessimism and depression. Instead, find the *ayāt* surrounding you and within you. Find meaning in everything. Be conscious of your gifts, your blessings, and all that is good in your life. Thank good people for being with you. Activism shouldn't just be about protest, it should preserve, beautify, and give hope.

What about experiencing doubts? When dealing with a Muslim struggling with doubts in his or her religion, you're not just dealing with the issue at hand. You're dealing with a flesh-and-blood person who is subject to culture, emotions, trauma, and other cognitive distortions. Doubt is a state of being, and it is not entirely mechanical. There have been many cases where people take their doubt to a teacher, and the teacher responds in a substantive, articulate way. But the doubter remains unsatisfied; or he simply comes back the next day with another doubt.

Finding the root issue is hard, but it is useless to keep chopping the weeds that asphyxiate the garden without uprooting them. The only way to find the root issue is to truly befriend and care for the person. I'll put it in more simple terms: you must follow the Sunna. This means you must be gentle, you must listen, you must be empathetic, and you cannot just strong-arm the person in a debate fashion.

Many Muslims these days are walking contradictions. They lack a knowledge of self, especially in a time when the media and pop culture is trying to get them away from their religion and cultures. There is also trauma – many Muslims have either witnessed conflict, or have relatives in unstable countries stricken by war, corruption, and poverty. Some become extreme in their religion, then experience "Salafi burnout" where they simply cannot maintain a strict lifestyle and perspective any longer

Later, you may find that the person has a certain influence in their life; or are grappling with a certain sin; or they are prone to hyper-skepticism, catastrophization, or overgeneralization. Maybe there is trauma at play. Maybe it is the culture. You can only find out once you know the person at their level – knees to knees, heart to heart.

Issues of mental health are very common today. Depression, anxiety, and behavioural disorders exist in every community. Complex problems must have multifaceted solutions. The first step is acknowledging the problem, and then treat the problem – but that is a big step that many prefer denying, and thus it gets worse. This is why I speak openly about my own mental health ups and downs – the taboos need to be broken if problems are expected to be fixed. In the meantime, let us make the absolute best out of our situations. All we have is right now.

Lavender is a floral herb that has long been used for aromatherapy. Its scent is calming, and it reduces anxiety. Taking even the slightest whiff of lavender will remind the anxious that tranquility can still be found in difficulty.

"Perhaps you hate a thing and it is good for you; and perhaps you love a thing and it is bad for you. And Allah Knows, while you know not." (2:216)

Chapter 6

Vanilla: Treating a Broken Heart

✳✳✳

The root ethic in Islam is maintaining a healthy heart. I'm not referring to the pulsating organ in your left chest, but rather I'm referring to the *qalb* described in so many verses in the Quran. The heart is the nexus that houses our intellect. It is the locus of our faith, the home of our innermost secrets, the intuitive criterion for good and evil, and the organ through which our Creator is known.

The root verb (قلب) means to turn, to flip, and to change. A healthy heart is soft: it fluidly changes from state to state, depending on its surroundings. If it perceives oppression, it expresses hatred for the oppressor and sympathy for the oppressed. If it perceives God's signs, it basks in wonder and amazement. If it perceives love, it loves. It is constantly reflecting and "turning", hence the root word. An unhealthy heart is a hard heart: it is numb, heavy, heedless, stagnant, and does not react to its surroundings. It is desensitized to good and evil, and it does not recognize God's signs. Its hardness impedes its ability to flux, which is what a heart is made to do.

The goal of Islamic ethics is to remain soft-hearted by practicing humility, by crying over injustice, to curb our arrogance and heedlessness, to be selfless, and to return to our natural order. Yes, having a soft heart can be painful, but those who turn their heart into a hard shell become bitter, distant, selfish, and absent-minded. A hard, heavy heart cannot flux, which is what a heart was made to do. Rather than genuinely turning their pain into a lesson, they mentally run away from their problems by locking their heart and letting nothing in. But only through heartfelt contemplation can true progress take place, both within yourself and within your society.

For some, the family is the basic unit of society. Family is seen as the building block of civilization, and the most basic natural association for the physical and emotional fulfillment of a people. For others, the individual is the basic unit of society, because individuals enjoy their own agency, even if they work towards a common end.

The basic unit of society in Islam, however, appears to be the heart. Being in a family is an ideal state, but it is not the reality for many people, nor is it *wājib*, nor does a family have complete agency. But similarly, to say that the individual is the basis is to assume that society is an amalgamation of separate, competing, selfish, and divergent people. The reality is that people are very connected – by blood, by tribe, by religion, by party, and by common interest. The heart in Islam does not deny the agency of the individual, but it is much more than individualism. It connects a person to his surroundings, and a cultivated heart is conscious of God and His signs.

And so the goal of a society should not just be productivity, because a productivity that ignores goodness is destructive. Rather, the goal of a society should be to maintain its humanity. A hard heart is vain, greedy, and heedless, while a soft heart is selfless, compassionate, and seeking constant betterment. If the basic unit is cultivated, our societal and political affairs will change overnight (13:11). Everything else in society – our families, our workplaces, our education, our entertainment, our religion, and our social lives – should all be geared towards maintaining and improving the basic unit of our society.

Don't put your heart in a fragile, glass box that is easily shattered. The shards will always hurt you. Rather, fill your heart with the remembrance of Allah. The remembrance of Allah is a semipermeable membrane that will protect your heart from certain dangers but open your heart to the right people and the right ideas. It is a vault whose combination is only accessed by the best of this world.

Faith increases and decreases. Its light leaves us when we sin, and it returns to us when we regain conscientiousness.

The worst state is one of heedlessness, where the heart neither remembers nor cares about its evil. The heedless heart avoids contemplating its reality and focuses on fleeting matters. This is called death in 6:122 of the Quran, because the heart no longer fluxes to your surroundings. First, you begin to sin privately whilst regretting the sin. Then, you sin privately, but you do not seek forgiveness. Next, you sin publicly, and make excuses for your behaviour. Finally, you sin publicly, and say that it is not a sin.

People that are in pain often inflict pain on others. They may be jaded misusers of people, they may be victims who feel schadenfreude at the suffering of others, they may be bringing their home environment to those on the outside, and they may be seekers of revenge. All the above is rooted in hard-heartedness. Hard-heartedness must be continually treated. It is like the common cold – it is not permanently cured, because it can keep coming back. So just as the cold is prevented and treated with a healthy regimen, the treatment of the hard heart is the continual contemplation of God, spending time with sanctified people, looking at creation and nature, reflecting on your own shortcomings and sins, moving yourself to forgive those who have harmed you, and helping the less fortunate. We are all keys being refined for the door to our Paradise.

A woman's love is so pure until it is misused by a thug. A man's love is so pure until it is misused by an exploiter. In reaction, we sometimes become exactly the person who took advantage of us. We make our hearts hard so that we don't feel the pain of being misused, or the guilt of using others. This is a coward's way out. We live in a time where everyone wants to be loved, but no one wants to admit their love to anyone else. Narcissism is in and devotion is a sign of weakness. "Love" became such an overused term that it is now either seen as cheesy, creepy, or fake. The users used it and the hard-hearted victims then avoided it afterward. Love is like kerosene. It can either be the fuel that builds civilization, or the fire that burns it down.

But there is a Lover (*al-Wadūd*) whose love only rewards. It brings relief to your heart in such an adverse world. All He asks for is mutuality. There is much to learn from His love that we should then carry into our own relationships. The first command was prostration: an act of veneration, submission, and selflessness – and the first disobedience was egotism.

When you remember your trials, always remember the trials of the Messenger of Allah ﷺ. Empathy for him is more virtuous than constantly feeling sorry for yourself. Moses asked Allah to expand his chest with reassurance, faith, and light (20:25). Allah fulfilled this prayer. But with Muḥammad ﷺ, Allah had already expanded his chest without him asking (94:1). He feared only his Lord, and thus, he maintained hope and grace in the most difficult of times. That is the nature of the Mercy to the Worlds.

To achieve humility, one must always exercise *sū'ath-thann* for his own self. Question your own intentions and be suspicious of your appetites. If someone compliments your character, assure yourself that they are just complimenting the veneer that Allah has put over their eyes. Remind yourself that Allah has hid many of your ills. "Humility is a strange thing – the minute you think you've got it, you've lost it."

The prophetic prescription for silence demonstrates a need to balance activity with repose. To give out energy by exerting and expressing yourself will prove to be exhausting and futile; unless matched by an equal and opposite degree of receptivity. The less you speak, the less you will be accounted for. You absorb your surroundings, learning and observing more. You rid the world of the binary dichotomy of subjects and objects and embrace its oneness.

The believers are in the world, but they are not of the world. They eat sparingly, they dress simply, limit their speech, lengthen their prayer, and constantly fight the appetites of their *nafs*. They may be alone in one sense, but they are alone with the Alone. Their company is one another, their home is the mosque, knowledge is their companion, scholars are their intimates, and the poor are their friends. Their tongues are constantly moving in *dhikr*. They are always busy, there is never a dull moment, because their hearts are in constant flux. So, what better company than your Lord and the believers? What better activity than the seeking of knowledge and adoration of the Beloved?

Even when experiencing the best that this world has to offer, there is always a sense of disturbance in my bones over the superficiality of material success. It's as subtle and as inconvenient as a splinter. When you try to quiet that disturbance with a higher dose of worldliness, the tastes of the *nafs* get more and more perverse. It gets to a point where you only wish to slay the beast rather than feed it with another offering from the depth of your soul. The next world is infinite and everlasting, this world is worth less than the wing of a fly. A ship sails best when it is on the water, without any punctures. If too much water enters the ship, the ship will sink. Likewise, you find success if you live in the *dunya* without letting the *dunya* live in you. If your heart is filled with this temporal world, it too will drown. Keep the *dunya* beneath your feet.

The social media world will always cheer harder the more perverse you are, the more vainglory you are, or the more skin is exposed. So, don't fall into Satan's trap, or else his demands will get weightier, and you lose the only part of you that you loved. If you take a picture of the full moon with your phone, that picture won't encapsulate its beauty. Likewise, you are not your pictures on social media. You can be so much more. The signs of Allah are around you and within you (41:53), and they all point to His magnificence. Be your true self, and not just a two-dimensional image.

While social media continuously rewards people for being provocative, making outrageous claims, and showing skin, dare to be different. Dare to have good character, dare to enjoin in the established virtues and prohibit evil, and dare to cover your outer beauty. The reward of maintaining your character outweighs the number of follows you have. Remember that Muḥammad ﷺ has over a billion followers, and he never even opened an account.

Hopelessness is a *bid'a*, At the bottom of Joseph's pit, he had nothing but Allah. And Allah brought him up from slavery to rulership. This is what the Quran calls the best of stories. Many African Americans are descendants of Muslim slaves. When those slaves saw their children being taken away and Christianized, they could not call on anyone but Allah. Four centuries later, 800,000 of those children rediscovered Islam in America, with very little help from the diaspora. Their forefathers called on Allah, so Allah called them back. Allah answers the prayer of the oppressed, even if after a while.

We're all broken – that's how the light gets in. We don't build for this world, we build for the Hereafter, so don't be melancholy if you don't see the immediate fruits of your labour. Your fruits will be ripe in Paradise. If you find yourself alone, maybe Allah wants some one-on-one time with you. If a man loses his vision, his hearing sharpens. Allah doesn't let you lose anything without giving you something else in return. "Surely with difficulty there is ease." (94:5)

The best medicine for the heart is love. What is love?

Love is Adam's repentance and apology to Allah.

Love is Noah's patience when calling his own disbelieving wife, son, and people for centuries.

Love is Ṣāliḥ offering the she-camel to his community.

Love is Jethro wanting economic justice for his community.

Love is Lot trying to get his people out of sin by offering his daughters in marriage.

Love is Allah taking Abraham as his Friend.

Love is Abraham's willingness to give his own firstborn son to God in sacrifice.

Love is Ishmael's patient obedience of his father's revelation.

Love is Jacob weeping for Joseph until he went blind.

Love is Joseph forgiving his brothers and reuniting with his family.

Love is Moses wanting to bring his people out of bondage and into guidance.

Love is Aaron wanting to keep the Israelites together to prevent schism.

Love is David reciting the Psalms for Allah with a beautiful voice in the midst of nature.

Love is Solomon desiring nothing but guidance from the Queen of Sheba – not her riches.

Love is John being dutiful to his parents and giving his life to Allah.

Love is Mary giving birth to and raising a child that she

never asked for.

Love is Jesus calling to the Israelites amidst their misguidance and persecution.

Love is Muḥammad's obsequiousness to God, and God taking him as His Beloved.

Love is Muḥammad calling to his people despite their wretched, foolhardy state.

Love is the believers preferring him over their own parents and their own selves.

– Peace be with them all.

Love is Allah creating the universe so that we may know His treasure.

Love is the demonstration and expression of our duty to Allah.

Love is the mercy and patience of the believers for one another.

Let's not forget love, but let's not misuse it either. Love is selflessness.

Chapter 7

Ginger Spice: Hurry to Success

***

Ginger is a sharp, peppery scent that simultaneously has a warmth and pleasance. It is used as a traditional medicine in many cultures to treat common illnesses. Likewise, we may be pierced with the thought of an impending responsibility, but it is in responsibility where we may find repose.

Doing nothing can be more stressful than working hard. When you're working hard, you're actualizing your human potential (*telos*) and witnessing the products of your achievement. The telos of an apple tree is a few hundred apples, feeding a few families for a few days. But the zenith of a human being is to be a Mercy to the Worlds ﷺ. In one hour, a tree can't even grow one apple, or move one step, or learn one word. But your potential for growth and upward mobility works on an hourly and minutely level. The progress and benefit that you can make is not quantifiable.

When you're procrastinating, or doing the minimum, you constantly live in the shadow of your potential self. You worry about the things you should be doing but aren't. You worry about your livelihood and future. Our sense of purpose is instilled within us, in the form of the things we know we need to do but are neglecting.

The Messenger ﷺ taught us to greet everyone with peace, to feed our hungry neighbours, to give a portion of our wealth in charity, to forgive those who harm us, to make excuses for those who trespass us, to seek knowledge from the cradle to the grave, to respect and honour all people, to avoid filling our stomachs with unnecessary foods, to abstain from substances that impair our judgment, to cease gossiping and backbiting, to refrain from judging others, to spend our nights praying to the Creator, and to protect our Earth and its precious resources from misuse and abuse.

Islam has always been a religion of duty. You can come as you are, but you cannot stay that way. The pillars of Islam are duties, *amr bil ma'rūf* is a duty, *da'wa* is a duty, and being a good spouse, neighbour, and friend is a duty. Jāhilīyya is the epitome of freedom from duty and ethics. But a completely free schedule and leisurely life is ultimately a stressful one, because there is nothing more taxing than a life without purpose. There is no growth in a care-free life with no schedule, no family, no commitments, and no work. These responsibilities tie us down, but they also build us up, fulfill us, and make us better people. No pain, no gain. Order is life, chaos is void.

In Jāhilīyya, the people were burying their daughters alive, neglecting orphans and widows, institutionalizing racism and tribalism, committing adultery, walking nakedly, and killing each other senselessly. But the Prophet Muḥammad ﷺ came with accountability, and that turned the entire world around. The belief in the Judgment puts consequences to people's actions. The inevitability of an end is what gives meaning to our time. It encourages us to go out and seek our livelihood, rather than sit around in perpetuity.

One of the most serious problems plaguing our people is laziness. There are missing initiatives, inactive or semi-active communities, a lack of punctuality, a lack of quality translations, a lack of readers, and intellectual stagnation. I of course speak of myself first before anyone else. The best advice I was given to defeat laziness was, "Small, consistent actions are better than big, inconsistent actions" (قليل مستمر ولا كثير منقطع). It is best to commit to daily progress, no matter how small, than to make hasty resolutions. My way of keeping my daily commitment is silly, but sometimes, I wear my watch or my ring on the wrong hand, and I only take it off once my responsibility is fulfilled. That way I won't forget, and I'll do it as soon as possible to relieve myself of a minor annoyance.

Motivation will burn at times and cool at other times, hence Islam puts so much stock in routine discipline.

Many of us struggle with our regular prayers. Prayer is a warm light that starts as a small spark. But once the habit develops, the light continues to radiate more and more, until it becomes a lantern that illuminates a dim world. Prayer starts as a seed, but with time, it grows into a luscious garden with an inviting fragrance. It was always difficult to get my students to pray. Hence, they need to be taught that ṣalāt will only help them when it is performed regularly. It is incremental and compounding in nature. Without watering a seed, it can never grow into a plant; and without maintaining a spark, it can never light up your world.

Allah gave Moses a miraculous staff, but Moses still had to throw the staff before it could become a serpent. Allah is ready to manifest miracles in your life – you just have to act: do your part, and let Him do the rest.

The nature of this world is that it is fleeting and distracting. But we were not created to have fun – we are allowed to have fun, but it has to be responsible fun. All too often, entertainment media is just another anesthetic that can potentially fill our minds with corruption. We could sit for hours alone just consuming it, while it normalizes promiscuity, gang culture, and recklessness to our conscious and unconscious self. They can entertain us till we drop dead – there is no end to it. Some will resort to intoxicants to avoid the stresses of the world. But your high should be in sobriety, not in intoxication; your trance should be in wisdom, not in stupidity; your fun should be in discovery, not in recovery. There is simply nothing of benefit to a substance that makes you nauseous, act stupid, poisons your liver, gives you hangovers, and puts you in a vulnerable position for predators. Your body rejects it, so your mind should too.

Iblīs comes at us from multiple directions: with idols, doubts, foods, drugs, entertainment, lethargy, and other forces of selfishness. And while these forces seem consequential to us, and may allure or frighten us, they are altogether just a house of cards. The deities and ideologies of the world are just ropes that are made to look like snakes. The magicians are just a clownish distraction. But once we cast what Allah has given us, all those false gods will be devoured, because Allah is God.

When we apply for a visa to a country, we make sure that our forms are filled out the right way. We follow all the rules and procedures, and we dot our i's and cross our t's on the application. So, what about your visa to Paradise? Is that something you'd like to half-ass, or will you try to do everything the right way? Your paradise or hell will be a reflection of your actions in this world. Are your actions beautiful or ugly? Are they fragrant or pungent? Are they sweet or bitter? You shall know a tree by its fruits.

Never lose sight of the ideal, even when it is not yet viable. If you were on an island with only pork available to eat, then you must eat pork in order to sustain your life. However, that does not mean that you should become satisfied with your ethical compromise. The second you see a bird, you should not say "well, I like pork, and I have become accustomed to it." You are obliged to abandon the exceptional ruling and return to the normative ruling. Your responsibility is to gradually make your actions the conduit of your highest ideals.

One of the greatest responsibilities that is incumbent upon us is to maintain respect at all times. Respect is the bridge that could bring competing rivals to reconciliation, warring factions to diplomacy, arguing spouses to resolution, and disagreeing friends to mutual admiration. Respect is a universal language that everyone understands. Everyone instinctively knows when they are not being respected. So, go back to those who have become distant from you. Smile, have long, endearing handshakes, ask about their family and health, and offer your help and assistance. Put away your phone and show them that you are listening. Relax your posture. Point out their goodness. One of the beautiful characteristics of the Prophet Muḥammad ﷺ is that he would face the person he was speaking to with his whole body. He would divide his attention equally among all his companions. He would never interrupt anyone. If we all took up these practices, we would greatly reduce all our communal troubles. The sacred is known through sanctified people.

Similarly, we must learn to respect words and language. We are accountable to the sharp and slithery products of our tongues. Allah distinguishes humans with their ability to articulate their thoughts and feelings (55:3-4). While some animals share some characteristics with humans, nothing can be compared to the complexity of human speech. When Moses became a prophet, he first prayed for the ability to speak clearly (20:25-28), and Allah granted that to him so that he may succeed in his mission. In return, Allah's favour on Moses was that He spoke directly to him (4:164).

Responsibility and persistence are key to lifting yourself up and finding success. But once you achieve a productive lifestyle, do not let it make you pompous. All who ripen must humbly remember that they were once raw, lest they rot.

Chapter 8

Peppermint: Diet and Wellness

***

Like the cool, sharp, refreshing scent of peppermint, one of the ways to maintain a sharp mind and a youthful body is through proper diet and nutrition. Taking care of your body is a part of Islam!

Prophet Muḥammad ﷺ encouraged you to only eat when you are hungry, and to stop eating before you are full. He encouraged you to only fill one third of your stomach with food and one third with beverages. He encouraged voluntary fasting long before the experts declared that it was healthy. He encouraged you to share your meals with your families, neighbours, and community. He encouraged you to seek natural remedies in healthy foods for common illnesses. He encouraged cleaning your teeth with every prayer. He mandated ablution with prayer and bathing on *jum'a*. He mandated a complete ban on all intoxicants. He remained slim and broad well into his 60s. He never obsessed over the [good or bad] taste of food. He encouraged archery, wrestling, racing, and horseback riding.

And yet, despite all of this, the rate of obesity is high in many Muslim countries. Our own scholars are often obese. I myself struggle with my weight.

Mastering the *nafs* is not only about abstaining from sin. It is about controlling your desires and never allowing them to override your intellect. When we admit that there is no god but Allah, we are to smash the idols that prevent us from Him. Those idols are not just statues of wood and stone, but greed, gluttony, and evil ideas too.

Instead of serving food with the "enjoy your meal!" attitude, serve it with the "good health and wellness!" (صحة وعافية) mentality. The former emphasizes the pleasureful component of food, while the latter emphasizes its sustenance. The reality is food is medicine. Too much medicine can be poison.

One of the great lessons of Ramadan is that the best can only be achieved through sacrifice. Good health requires us to sacrifice our gluttony and tame our appetites. The original Adamic test was over a morsel of food. In many respects, the same test is manifest in our lives today: what we consume, of food or ideas, will either build us or cause us to perish.

Stores always put the chocolates, the chips, and the gossip magazines on your way to the cashier. Your best interest is to focus on your graceful exit. This is a similitude for the *dunya*. There are plenty of temptations, but we're all on our way out and it is better to stay focused on that.

May we return to a life of healthy eating, regular fasting, exercise and strength; and move away from the high sugar, carbs, grease, salt, and calorie diets of modernity.

Chapter 9

Blue Orchid: Family is Forever

***

"When you like a flower, you pick it. When you love a flower, you water it."

You will not marry Mr. Perfect or Miss Perfect.

Every human being was born with the instinct to seek Perfection. We seek perfection in our appearance, our words, our grades, our jobs, our parents, our spouses, our power... in everything. We look frantically for it, but we don't know what it is. Sometimes, we think we found it – perhaps in a partner – until we understand that there must be something more perfect than this. We see flaws everywhere.

We don't really understand Perfection, but we want it more than anything. That Perfection is God. We are all born upon the *fitra*, knowing Him. We all bore witness to Him Alone in the previous world. But we have fallen, looking for every sign and every trace that can take us back to Him. To God we belong, and to Him we will return.

One trap of bachelorhood is in waiting for the "perfect" spouse, so we ignore the real people in front of us. But marriage in the Quran is a force of healing. Prophet Lot wanted the best for his people, and so he offered his daughters in marriage, so that they may be taken out of the state of sin (11:78). The wives of Noah and Lot were also sinners (66:10). Chapter 66 of the Quran also addresses the domestic issues of the Prophet Muḥammad ﷺ.

The prophets were spiritual doctors. They sought to rectify those around them. Prophet Muḥammad ﷺ married older women, women with children, and widows, not because they were good enough for him, as he truly does not have any equal. He married them so that he may help them. So instead of only helping yourself, find someone whom you can bring closer to Allah.

That being said, do not marry a person expecting them to change. There may be some core characteristics in your partner that will stay static over the course of their life.

While you can mutually help one another reduce some negative qualities, the only person you truly have power to change is yourself – and even that is a trying task. Few can properly diagnose a psychological or spiritual illness, let alone treat it. When selecting a spouse, you must maintain enough criteria to maintain your physical, psychological, and spiritual safety. Otherwise, a marriage can easily turn into a battlefield.

One may ask, "Why should I get married if I'm happy? I have God." That same God said that He created us in pairs (51:49), that spousal love is a sign of Him (30:21), that spouses are the garments of one another (2:187), and that a wife is a man's tilth (2:223). Marriage brings one closer to Allah.

Yes, marriage is an immense responsibility. But I can't think of a more rewarding and worthwhile responsibility than the upkeep of a human being. If we were meant to remain single, then Allah would not have programmed us biologically, psychologically, and chemically in the way that He did; and He would have just had us reproduce asexually. Instead, we are moved to discover the yin-yang of male and female relationships, so that we may become more selfless, more mature, more patient, and more responsible – the qualities of a true believer.

At the very least, one should marry to leave the state of sin and enter the state of purity. We all have sins of the eyes, sins of the tongue, or sins of the physical body. Protect yourselves and your religion.

There will always be exceptions – even among some of our prophets, scholars, and *awliyā*'. But those are exceptions. Marriage is on the decline worldwide, and single parenthood is quickly becoming the norm in parts of the world. A society cannot function without stable families and a certain birth rate.

The Quran delineates three keys to a successful marriage: *sakīna* (7:189), *mawadda* and *raḥma* (30:21). *Sakīna* is tranquility, and one must find a partner with whom he or she is at ease with. The marital home should be a place of peace, where a person returns to recharge their mental and spiritual battery. *Mawadda* is a mutual demonstration of love, which must persist even after the honeymoon phase is over. Love cannot just be expressed through intimacy – it must be continually demonstrated in duty and in true beauty. *Raḥma* is mercy, beneficence and compassion. Every marriage has straws, and you must learn to forgive the shortcomings of your partner and forget their rectified errors. Be to others as you want Allah to be to you – Gracious and Merciful.

Respect is the bedrock of every relationship. There will be times where you feel that you do not love your partner. In those situations, you should never belittle them, curse at them, ignore them, share their secrets, hit them, or attack their self-esteem. Even if you are at the cusp of divorce, you should see your partner as a human being that deserves respect and give them their *ḥaq*. Respect is the one thing that is mandatory, and if it is not there, then the marriage is bound to destroy itself.

One of the objects of starting a family is having children. Motherly love is both the most universal and the most singular. Yet, the importance of family is waning from the minds of many. The family has been effectively replaced by the individual as the basic unit of society. Notice how the most consequential Enlightenment thinkers did not have any children: Hobbes, Locke, Rousseau, Spinoza, Voltaire, Kant, Hume, John Stuart Mill, and Adam Smith did not have children. Many other influential modern thinkers had similar family issues: Marx, Nietzsche, Darwin, and Freud.

Perhaps the lack of a family precipitated the radical individualism that they helped create. Genuine fatherhood is supposed to make a man committed and selfless, and put the needs of his wife, family, tribe, and country before his own. It ties you down to responsibilities; while the Enlightenment ideals are all about expanding individual agency. Family is a cornerstone of the Abrahamic religions. Is this why modern society is producing increasingly childish men, who aren't marrying, producing children, attending church, and are now falling behind in academics and business? Are they simply channeling the values of their progenitors?

We live in a time where the uniqueness of motherhood and fatherhood is being pushed aside in favour of an androgynous model parenthood. Even then, the state is now becoming the primary protector, provider, and teacher of children.

Regardless of the promises of prosperity that modernism boasts, we must always be fixated on the only certainty in life: death. The *adhān* for our funeral prayer is called in our ear when we are born. This world is just a short break in between. There is a brief break in between the *adhān* and the prayer — some perform their *nāfila*, some recite *duʿāʾ*, some read Quran, some reflect silently. Well, this Earth is a mosque too, so spend your brief time performing good deeds and reflecting. With this mindset, you will not waste precious family time with pettiness. You will seize the moment and see your partner in perspective: that we belong to God, and your partnership will only continue in Paradise if the two of you have committed yourself to faith and good works.

Do not forget your parents after marriage – they started you on this journey of life, and they brought you up from helplessness to strength. If you're regularly calling your parents and in-laws, visiting them, serving them, and speaking about them in a positive manner, then your kids will usually subconsciously pick up these habits as well. If you roll your eyes at your parents, then expect your kids to do the same.

Even if your family is not practicing, recite the Quran beautifully in your home. Invite them to join you in prayer. Forgive their faults, give them gifts, obey them in goodness, restrain your anger toward them, and speak calmly and gently. Show them that Islam has made you the best version of yourself.

Lastly, remember your spiritual family. "The believers are but brothers" (49:10). What's missing in our lives is not just good spousal relationships, but brotherhood and sisterhood bonds. When the Messenger made brotherhood bonds between his companions, the Commander of the Faithful ʿAlī b. Abī Ṭālib came with tears in his eyes, saying, "O Messenger of Allah! You have made brotherhood bonds among your companions, but you have not made a brotherhood bond between me and anyone!" So, the Messenger replied, "I am your brother in this world and the Hereafter."[16]

This brotherhood was acted upon all throughout their lives. Muḥammad ﷺ named ʿAlī in the cradle, and ʿAlī was the first man to follow the Prophet after he was commissioned. ʿAlī was the only one who stood up and supported the Messenger at Daʿwat Dhul ʿAshīra. ʿAlī was the one who slept in the Messenger's bed when the Quraysh were hunting him down.

ʿAlī b. Abī Ṭālib was sent to the front lines of Badr. He was the one who would be chosen to marry the Prophet's daughter, the Mistress of the Women of the Worlds. He and Abu Dujānah were the only men accompanying the Messenger at Uḥud. ʿAlī was the only one brave enough to fight ʿAmr b. ʿAbd al-Wud at Khandaq. ʿAlī negotiated and wrote the Treaty of Hudaybīya, and refused to cross out the sentence "Muḥammad the Messenger of Allah." ʿAlī was appointed to rule over Medina, like Aaron, in the Messenger's expedition to Tabuk. ʿAlī was sent to guide the people of Yemen.

When the Messenger ﷺ returned to Mecca to break the idols, ʿAlī stood on top of his holy shoulders, grabbed the

---

أَنْتَ أَخِي فِي الدُّنْيَا وَالآخِرَةِ ¹⁶

largest idol on top of the Kāʿba, and tossed it onto the ground.

Imam ʿAlī was once asked if he was a prophet. So he replied, "Woe to you! Surely, I am only a servant from the servants of Muḥammad."[17]

In all the above examples, we see that ʿAlī b. Abī Ṭālib loved the Prophet ﷺ more than he loved himself. Not only did he regularly put his life on the line for the sake of his Beloved ﷺ, but he never viewed these actions as favours. He saw his service to Muḥammad ﷺ as a means to get closer to Allah. It was unconditional love for an older brother, a shaykh, a role model ...

If you don't have a good brother that is by your side, who understands you and knows your pain, who is a real friend to you, then you're missing out in life. There is great joy in serving your brother, and great joy in being served by your brother. Just make sure that your brother or sister is someone who will make you better. We will all be raised with those whom we love. May Allah raise us with the Master of Messengers, his righteous and pure family, and his shining and goodly companions.

"A brother of a brother is a brother." Islam is the biggest family in the world. Value your Muslim friendships: they

---

17 ويلك، إنما أنا عبد من عبيد محمد صلى الله عليه واله وسلم. يعني بذلك: عبد طاعته لا غير ذلك

started at the Primordial Covenant, and they will end in the highest heaven. Family is forever – God-willingly.

Sandalwood: Rethinking Islamic Education

***

Sandalwood has a distinctive warm, woody scent. It is piney, like fresh-cut wood with a hint of varnish. It is rich, deep, and powerful – like knowledge. The Quran compares a good word to a good tree (14:24), and education turns the tree into a furnished home.

A few years ago, we waited in the mosque for our shaykh to come lead us in Maghrib prayer. We tarried for about five minutes, until he came rushing in. He saw that we had not yet prayed, so he called the *iqāma* and led us. After the prayer and *tasbīḥ*, he turned to us and said, "There are two leadership models: that of the geese, and that of the bulls. Geese take turns leading the flock, while bulls scatter when they lose the leader of the pack. If I'm not here for prayers on time, then select one from among yourselves to lead the prayers."

A good leader is able to build the infrastructure of an organization, and he or she spends extra time, money, and effort doing so. A teacher is also a leader – but a teacher's job is not to build an organization, it is to build people. Like a good leader, a teacher should be able to prepare students for their inevitable independence. Students are the future leaders, and thus a teacher-student relationship is a mutually beneficial one. It is the key to intergenerational progress. When we are ill and elderly, they will be our caretakers.

A leader's job is to cultivate citizens, not slaves. Likewise, the job of a teacher is not to create sycophants. A school must create scholars.

The teacher-student relationship is a sacred one. The Prophet had a teacher: Angel Gabriel. The Prophet was of higher status than the angel, but he still honoured him and humbled himself before him. Allah did not need to create Gabriel. There was no need for this medium between Him and His Servant ﷺ. But perhaps Allah is teaching us through this example that our knowledge should be taken from a teacher and transmitted from one mouth to another.

Despite specializing in political science, I always knew that education was my passion. An educator will never put a policy in place, but he or she can transform the lives of thousands of people. Knowledge is an immaterial inheritance that we possess for a little while before passing it on. The transmigration of knowledge is billions of years old. There is no possession of the prophets that is more valuable.

Reflect on the life of Jāʿfar b. Muḥammad as-Ṣādiq سلام الله عليه. He is remembered for his contributions to *fiqh*, *hadīth*, and even the natural sciences (he taught chemistry to Geber, the Father of Chemistry). Because of his noble lineage and scholastic prominence, he was constantly invited to lead revolutions against the Umayyads; and to meet other dissidents in Kūfa. Jāʿfar as-Ṣādiq always refused, and even burned their letters, because he knew that many of the rebels were only interested in worldly affairs. He preferred to spend his life teaching in Medina, at the Mosque of our Prophet ﷺ where he had thousands of students from all over the world.

Now, people barely know the names of the rulers of his time. We don't even know some of the names and biographies of the rebel leaders. The riches of these sultans don't matter anymore. But the legacy of Jāʿfar lives on, and his work has been immortalized in the legal schools and the books of *hadīth*.

An effective teacher leads by example, not merely by words. We must say much with few words. The Messenger of Allah ﷺ said that he had been commissioned with "succinct language" (جوامع الكلم); expressions that are comprehensive yet condensed, designed to deliver full meanings with few words. As a Prophet with a weighty assignment, he made sure that his words were unambiguous and direct, yet eloquent and nuanced at the same time. So ideally, teachers should learn to speak less and act more, because your actions are more poignant.

Lecturing is not very affective – it's easy for the audience to zone out or forget the substance of the lecture. Even adults find it difficult to sit through a ten-minute speech, so how do you think kids feel; especially those with attention deficit? Can we even recount the last three sermons that we have heard in any detail? Once, the Prophet was upset that his companions were not following his orders to make a sacrifice after they were denied from Hajj. His wife Umm Salama advised him to go ahead and make the sacrifice himself, in hope that the companions would follow suit. So, he sacrificed his animal, then the companions did the same.

Be extra patient with your students' questions. When the Prophet was taken up on the *mi'rāj*, he was introduced to the heavens and to knowledge that we cannot begin to fathom. Then, he was brought back to this mundane world, and had to deal with people that barely had knowledge of this plane. It was like an advanced calculus professor teaching children how to add and subtract. Yet, the Messenger was patient and kind, and reformed his people over decades. We must teach in accordance to the ability of our students; as Messenger Muḥammad ﷺ said, "We, the community of prophets, speak to the people in accordance to the level of their intellect."[18]

As teachers, all we can really do is outline the basics, whilst simultaneously accommodating everyone with our very divided attention. A student that is only focused on the curriculum and their grades may not develop the inspiration or the critical thinking skills needed to become scholastic learners. So, find a discipline that your students or your kids are passionate about, and have them commit to regular progress on it. Make sure that progress is properly scheduled and measurable. Sometimes, the best way to do this is by starting a project that has a clear product cycle — like writing (or translating) a book from beginning to end, for example. This way, during the project, they will learn what skills they need to develop and work on in an organic way. Most importantly, teach them to put Allah first in their learning. He is a Cause that never ceases, unlike our grades, our degrees, our jobs, and our parents' approval.

Don't just give your children and students criticism. Make sure you are telling them what they are doing right. Praise their effort and compliment their good work. If all you do is criticize, then they will learn to avoid you, hide their mistakes from you, and wean away from seeking your stingy validation. The Messenger was not just a Warner (*nadhīr*), he came with glad tidings (*bashīr*) first and

---

18 نحن معاشر الأنبياء أمرنا أن نكلم الناس على قدر عقولهم

foremost. He never walked away from his people, despite the savagery of their condition.

Integrating Islamic ethics into everyday school subjects should be the goal of every Muslim teacher. Modern secular academia often operates on naturalist assumptions, hyper-skepticism, and liberal biases. Academia operates as though the spiritual is just imaginative, and so it is purely a worldly analysis. Very few academics effectively challenge this framework, but even they must usually work within it. When you approach any religious topic from a naturalist lens, you are denying it of its supernatural potential, and mostly focusing on its socio-economic and anthropological value.

Academia today can be likened to studying the sewer system, but without ever acknowledging that there is a world above the ground. If we don't acknowledge who built the sewer, where the matter comes from, and the universe above the underground, then our study will be limited and blind.

Our focus should be teaching our children interdisciplinary problem-solving. We often compartmentalize our subjects: we only talk about science in Science Class, or we only talk about art in Art Class. Students then develop a preference of one subject over another. In reality, students should be made to solve complex problems that involve different faculties of their brain. A lesson on medicine could be complemented with a discussion on ethics. A math word-problem could incorporate scenarios from history class. Eastern education systems involve a lot of rote memory. While the students learn to be disciplined and studious, they often fail to develop critical thinking skills, intellectual curiosity, and interpersonal intelligence.

Due to rapid technological advancements, we are preparing children today for jobs that may not currently exist. Automation is set to replace most jobs, and new industries and ventures will pop up. The basis of entrepreneurship and innovation is creative problem-solving.

In the end, we don't teach for the income. We teach for the outcome.

Chapter 11

Rosemary: Remembering Divine Justice

***

The highest station in Islam is to love what Allah loves and to dislike what Allah dislikes.

Standing up for what is right requires tremendous fortitude. The prophets lost their homes, their families and their lives because they voiced an unpopular opinion. We Muslims are up against modern Pharaohs on every side of the political spectrum. Out of fear, some Muslims look for powerful allies in the Pharaonic system, hoping that they will find some comfort in this life. But the true Muslim is one who fears none but God – that is the highest degree of *tawḥīd*. Once you understand the metaphysical consequences of all things, you'll be able to speak in Pharaoh's court without your voice shaking and without your joints trembling.

Some of us will lose our friends, our jobs, our family, our freedom, or even our lives for this work. But as the Quran says, "Surely, my prayer, my sacrifices, my life and my death are for Allah, Lord of the Worlds." (6:162)

One may ask, what does Islam have to do with social justice politics? The answer: one must not separate politics from ethics, and Islam has much to say on ethics. You can't compartmentalize "religion" to just being a daily meditation, a weekly temple attendance, and an annual commemoration. Separating politics from religion is like separating biology from psychology. Our minds may put the two in different categories to simplify or systematize knowledge and information, but the two are interrelated and interdependent. Humans have a way of organizing and categorizing different ideas, but that does not change that life is just one big cauldron with all the ingredients mixed in: psychology, biology, sociology, anthropology, spirituality, politics, and more.

On that note: modern capitalist economics is now seldom related to ethics, even though ethics should be the foundation of every political and economic system. Free market capitalism today is seen simply as glorified bookkeeping – a mathematical process designed to increase efficiency and productivity. Discussions on ethics are usually anecdotal exercises to keep the classroom interesting, but ultimately, the market is a utilitarian machine. Most of the ethical problems of capitalism are sidelined due to the great wealth that it has produced. Sure, we cannot deny that it has surpassed the slave-driven and feudal models, both in standard of living and in efficiency, as it has vastly improved the quality of life of all people [albeit not in an egalitarian way]. But capitalism has brought about new and unprecedented forms of destruction through ecological damage, the military-industrial complex, factory farming, private prisons, brain drain in the developing world, processed foods, dangerous new technologies, the sex industry, and other kinds of legal exploitation.

A market must always be guided by rules. In the same way that regulations exist in business, ethical regulations need to be extended to prevent self-destructive behavior. Capitalist democracies cannot always create protocols against behaviours that are deeply ingrained in societies, because people will not always vote against the interests of their egos and appetites.

While capitalism has produced more wealth than any other system, quality of life is determined by more than just the accumulation of capital. A new German study suggests that Muslims have the highest life satisfaction in the world – even higher than Christians, Buddhists, and yogis.[19] Suicide rates in the Muslim world are generally lower even in comparison to wealthy European, North American, and East Asian countries. In Islam, quiet of

---

[19] https://www.dailymail.co.uk/health/article-6908769/Muslims-highest-life-satisfaction-thanks-feeling-oneness.html

mind is found in the remembrance of God (13:28), and the good life is the product of good works (16:97).

The pursuit of an ethical society is not the same as the pursuit of political expediency. We must be trained to look to what is best for civilization. Politics and civilization are not the same. Something may be good for politics, but not good for civilization. While legalizing illegal substances may be good for recreation and taxation, such substances do not build up civilization. They keep us stagnant and distracted at best; and can cause serious illnesses and social decay at worst.

The word for "politics" in Arabic is "*siyāsa*" (سياسة). Its root word is "*sawasa*", which means "to tend, to manage". It is etymologically connected to the Semitic word "*sus*", which means "horse", and the word was originally used in bedouin society to refer to the tending and training of beasts. Hence, a *sā'is* was a manager or trainer of horses and camels. The Prophet Muḥammad ﷺ said, "The Children of Israel were led (*tasūsuhum*, same word as *siyāsa*) by prophets: Whenever a prophet died, another would take over his place."[20] Thus, the literal purpose of politics is to civilize people and train us to avoid behaving with our base instincts. A righteous leader makes us better humans and helps us to realize our *fiṭra*, which is rooted in goodness. The prophets and the *awliyā'* sought to make good people out of their nations. It is only disorder and oppression that brings evil out of us. Our political criteria as Muslims should never simply be "as long as it doesn't

---

20 إِنَّ بَنِي إِسْرَائِيلَ كَانَتْ تَسُوسُهُمْ أَنْبِيَاؤُهُمْ كُلَّمَا ذَهَبَ نَبِيٌّ خَلَفَهُ نَبِيٌّ

hurt anybody", because that criteria will always miss the true purpose of politics – elevation, not stagnation and not degeneration.

All Muslims should be involved in establishing justice in their families, schools, workplaces and societies. It's not enough to maintain a "Muslim identity" or "Muslim culture". Abu Lahab, the uncle of the Prophet ﷺ who was damned in the Quran, was a man of great status and lineage. He was rich, handsome, proud and unapologetic. By today's definition, Abu Lahab looked "Muslim", spoke Arabic, ate Middle Eastern food, and wore Arabian clothing. Yet, he was damned with his own chapter of the Quran. On the other hand, companions like Salman and Bilal received the high praise of the Prophet ﷺ. Being "Muslim-ish "is the new norm among a certain class of Muslim immigrants. They look and identify as Muslims, but they have forgotten that Islam is a process. It's not just about being a brown-skinned medical professional or engineer. It's about submission to something bigger than yourself, trusting God (*imān*), being conscious of God, and eventually, knowing God.

Establishing justice does not always mean rebelling against existing power structures. Not every revolution is good – the first to revolt, after all, was Satan. Many in the activist circles see revolution as the pre-eminent solution to even the slightest of grievances. They simplistically divide the world into two camps, "dominant" and "marginalized"; and they pit various quasi-tribal identities against one another in perpetuity. At first site, such a schema appears compassionate, as it may give a voice to persecuted

104

peoples. But this system comes with the exact same assumptions about the world that the dominant system has: (1) the belief that the world is controlled by power and chance, (2) the belief that truth is relegated to the observable natural sciences, (3) the belief that pre-modern spirituality is superstitious and ritualistic, (4) the belief that suffering is all evil, all natural, and does not have meaning, (5) and no formal end-goal or salvation, unlike Islam. When all is said and done, they ultimately put their faith in the free market, and fall back onto Anglo-Saxon individualist naturalist liberalism.

Some of these activists take aim at the Islamic tradition itself. They wish to reform Islam, and they assume that we today are more enlightened than our prejudiced forefathers, that the Islamic sciences are fundamentally broken, that traditionalism is in every way more restrictive or primitive, and that humans arrogate their own rights. Instead of pursuing "reform" – which is to say that Islam has become obsolete or outdated – we should be pursuing *tajdīd* and *islah*.

The words *tajdīd* and *islah*, which were used by the Messenger ﷺ and Imam al-Husayn respectfully, do not mean "reform" – neither in their strict dictionary definitions nor in their feelings evoked. *Islah* means to rectify, and to bring something back to its intended state and function. *Tajdīd* means to renew or to renovate, but not necessarily to add new ingredients and components. Within the vast (and vastly unread) Islamic tradition is everything needed to renovate and rectify our practice. This religion at its core, including its legal tradition, is flexible to time, space, and context. It has everything we need to revitalize our practice and redress our problems. Reformism, on the other hand, can only lead to nihilism, cosmic despair, moral relativity, extremism, and the overspreading darkness of Satan.

Historically, rosemary was considered the scent of remembrance. It was said to have improved one's memory; and it was used in funerals and war commemoration. It is pungent and aromatic. One of the reasons why many Muslims seek innovative solutions to our problems is because our people have endured immeasurable trauma. It's hard to point at a part of the Muslim world that isn't facing tough times. It's rare to meet a Muslim who has not been directly or indirectly affected by a recent conflict. We cannot betray our dead by forgetting about them. They should always be in our supplications. We need to learn from their bravery and continue to stand for the ideals that they died for. Their blood may be cheap to some, but each drop of their blood is more valuable to God than the riches of the world.

We need to wake up to this calculated effort to subvert the Muslim world. This is our holocaust. The past 100 years has been our Century of Shame (百年国耻), and it's time we put an end to it – by God's permission.

The Muslim world may be the underdog, but so was King David. He defeated the much larger Goliath with a simple slingshot. Allah granted him a mighty kingdom, yet that honour was paired with his legendary prostration (38:24), his obsequious supplication (21:79), and his bi-daily fast. Allah only elevates a servant once he realizes how lowly he is before God. The direction we seek is not right, not left, not progressive, not backward. The direction is up, the goal is to uplift. We were made for ascension, not for the Fall and not for stagnation.

Chapter 12

Citrus Paradisi: A Humble Ascent after the Fall

***

Citrus Paradisi, better known as grapefruit, is the only citrus fruit that doesn't originate from the Old World. In the 18th century, Reverend Griffith Hughes was on a quest of finding the Tree of Knowledge from the Garden of Eden. Unusual orange fruits hanging from the lush green branches of the Caribbean struck his attention. They seemed to resemble the legendary "golden apples" from the story of Adam. While it may not truly be the "forbidden fruit", its peel is widely used in aromatherapy. It is today one of the most widely-used ingredients in citrussy perfumes.

Some Muslims have started to have doubts about the story of creation as narrated in the noble Quran after reading about evolution. Prior to Darwin's theory of evolution, the Muslim civilization was usually not keen on hindering scientific progress, and in fact did much to propel it. With modern evolutionary biology however, there appears (at least on the surface) to be a clash between science and scripture. What are the forces at play here? What variables must be considered when dealing with this problem?

The common stem from which these doubts sprout is an epistemology grounded in naturalism. The scientific method obviously has a place in truth-seeking: it draws its conclusions from sensory observation and gives us indubitable truths about the universe in which we live. One should not abandon the scientific method as a tool in the quest to understand reality, but it is a tool, nonetheless. Science is always at the drawing board, revising old research, devising new methods, and challenging old conclusions. The basis of science is reason, which is why an experiment begins with a hypothesis (an educated guess of what we logically expect to take place) and a null hypothesis (what we expect will not take place). This presupposes cause and effect, and the law of non-contradiction; the idea that our universe operates in an orderly way, and that events do not happen at random. In the same way that logic is the foundation of science, it is also the foundation of our *kalāmi* arguments for the existence of God.

The scientific method as a tool will not be able to answer every question on ethics, anthropology, cosmology, purpose, metaphysics, consciousness, life, being, and epistemology – and although these areas are more uncertain and immaterial than the hard sciences, they are ultimately what we live for. So, when one sees New Atheists dismiss philosophy, or religion, this is quite naive, because philosophy is the incorporeal foundation of science, and religion is the incorporeal foundation of society; with science being a tool with its own scope. New Atheism merely grew out of the carcass of occidental Christianity, and its logical conclusion is postmodernism, which is nihilistic, hedonistic, confused, and suicidal.

So, with that in mind, when science, which is sensory observation with inconclusive fluidity, becomes the criterion by which convention is confirmed or denied, there will naturally be clashes. Sometimes, those clashes exist only in the mind, because they are a clash between an interpretation of convention and a perceived reality. Other times, the clash can be based on flawed or incomplete scientific research. I do not deny evolution per se. But there are gigantic discoveries that occur periodically, discoveries that challenge previously held beliefs in evolution and clash with existing hypotheses, discoveries that may have their own flaws, which may be exposed with the next discovery. This is partly why one finds it difficult to answer questions on evolution; it is like the Big Bang: some are quick to find references to the Big Bang in the Quran and *ḥadīth*, but if the Big Bang theory were ever superseded by science (and alternative hypotheses do exist), then that would throw those interpretations out as well. What this writer has realized after studying at three universities is that these educational institutions have their own faith-based biases, assumptions, and ideologies, which guide their research – this is far more pronounced in the social sciences of course, but not necessarily limited to them.

Ultimately, we won't achieve 100% scientific certainty in either the present evolutionary conclusions or in the Adamic story. This then poses a question: is there any conventional value to the Adamic story? Whether or not it physically took place (and I believe that it did, in some way or another), it is an origin story that has resonated with billions of people worldwide for thousands of years, with profound psychological truths and practical sociological lessons. Of course, the Islamic version is a bit more in line with naturalistic thinking – with the worldly setting of the story, the earthly origins of mankind, no mention of timeline and genealogy, and no "original sin". There are even traditions of there being many "Adams". But, one has to go deeper into the story. The Quran avoids historicizing events, and so it lacks many dates, names, and places, and instead, encourages us to reflect on the lessons taught in each story.

On one side, the story talks about humanity's viceregency of God on Earth, humanity's ability to comprehend the ʿaql, and humanity's eloquent mastery of language; on the other side, it talks about humanity's naivety, its base desires, and the sorrow after its fall. The story highlights the dualistic nature of man: that we are both celestial in one sense and earthly in another; spiritual and physical, supernatural and natural, "human" and animal. It is a story about the great natural telos of man, followed by his tragic fall, followed by his humble ascent. On another level, it talks of humanity's common, meek, and worldly origin, to avoid tribalism, racism, and chauvinism.

This same story is reflected in mankind both on a microcosmic and macrocosmic level. We all have our own individual falls, where we immaturely decline into heedlessness. But on a civilizational level, we continue to fall vertically, from holistic celestial worldviews to our base desires. Philosophically, we have fallen from religious philosophy (philosophy of the spiritual hierarchy), to rational philosophy, to naturalist philosophy, to contemporary relativism (philosophy of the base human self, under the guise of "identity").

The problem with the evolutionary worldview is that it views mankind simply as bonafide tool-making animals. Evolution replaced the perennial notion of man's fall with a theory of material progress. It gives us the illusion of progress. But the reality is that we are falling from the divine to the mundane. The Christian world went from the leadership of prophets, to apostles, to false apostles, to pseudo divine kings, to secular materialist rulers, to the current White House spectacle. They went from traditional Christianity, to Protestantism, to capitalism and socialism, to modern identities based on our diet, sexual preferences, and gender identity.

The Muslims went through a similar fall, from corrupt dynasties, to colonialism, to militant secular states, to

112

chaos. While this time is certainly noted for the rise of its science and technology, we can see mankind falling into dogmatism, nihilism, social decadence, frivolity, vanity, impatience, and depression. Jāhilīyya was a Fall to the bottom, from where the Prophet ﷺ brought his people back up. The *aḥadīth* describe the degeneracy of the End Times, but the night is darkest just before the dawn, and as soon as even the dimmest of light appears on the horizon, the very nature of people will pull them toward it – the Mahdi and Jesus.

In this sense, conventional truths, which are the sifted and sieved amalgamation of human thought and experience, have a meta-historical archetypal nature that is often more authentic than sensory truths. It would be foolish to disregard either one, because one deals with how, and the other deals with why. With a purely evolutionary worldview, man is a tool-making animal, and our progress as a species is measured in the linear paradigm of scientific and technological advancement. But this says little about our quality of life, purpose of life, why we live, how we should live, where we come from, what it means to be human, the power of thought and conscious experience, and whether we really are "better" or more developed than our ancestors. It gives the illusion of upward ascent, but I see a downward regression during what should be humanity's most enlightened time, and that regression comes from our killing of our father – tradition, convention, religion, and ritual.

The Fall gives meaning to human anxiety, depression, and alienation; and a promise of an ascent through effort,

113

hope, promise, responsibility, and a return to being, viceregency, and sainthood.

May Allah protect us from the evil hidden within ourselves, "and from the evil of darkness when it overspreads" (113:3).

Made in the USA
Las Vegas, NV
08 September 2022

54884215R00069